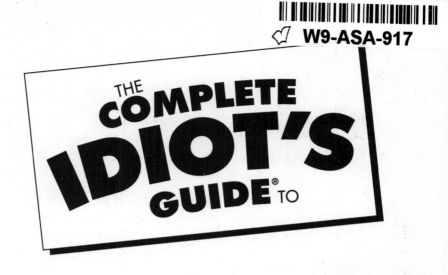

THE
COMPLETE
IDIOT'S
GUIDE® TO

Chess Openings

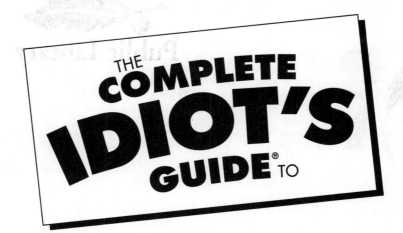

Chess Openings

by William Aramil

ALPHA

A member of Penguin Group (USA) Inc.

ALPHA BOOKS

Published by the Penguin Group

Penguin Group (USA) Inc., 375 Hudson Street, New York, New York 10014, USA

Penguin Group (Canada), 90 Eglinton Avenue East, Suite 700, Toronto, Ontario M4P 2Y3, Canada (a division of Pearson Penguin Canada Inc.)

Penguin Books Ltd., 80 Strand, London WC2R 0RL, England

Penguin Ireland, 25 St. Stephen's Green, Dublin 2, Ireland (a division of Penguin Books Ltd.)

Penguin Group (Australia), 250 Camberwell Road, Camberwell, Victoria 3124, Australia (a division of Pearson Australia Group Pty. Ltd.)

Penguin Books India Pvt. Ltd., 11 Community Centre, Panchsheel Park, New Delhi—110 017, India

Penguin Group (NZ), 67 Apollo Drive, Rosedale, North Shore, Auckland 1311, New Zealand (a division of Pearson New Zealand Ltd.)

Penguin Books (South Africa) (Pty.) Ltd., 24 Sturdee Avenue, Rosebank, Johannesburg 2196, South Africa

Penguin Books Ltd., Registered Offices: 80 Strand, London WC2R 0RL, England

Copyright © 2008 by William Aramil

International Standard Book Number: 978-1-59257-776-7
Library of Congress Catalog Card Number: 2008924715

10 09 08   8 7 6 5 4 3 2 1

Interpretation of the printing code: The rightmost number of the first series of numbers is the year of the book's printing; the rightmost number of the second series of numbers is the number of the book's printing. For example, a printing code of 08-1 shows that the first printing occurred in 2008.

Printed in the United States of America

Note: This publication contains the opinions and ideas of its author. It is intended to provide helpful and informative material on the subject matter covered. It is sold with the understanding that the author and publisher are not engaged in rendering professional services in the book. If the reader requires personal assistance or advice, a competent professional should be consulted.

The author and publisher specifically disclaim any responsibility for any liability, loss, or risk, personal or otherwise, which is incurred as a consequence, directly or indirectly, of the use and application of any of the contents of this book.

Most Alpha books are available at special quantity discounts for bulk purchases for sales promotions, premiums, fund-raising, or educational use. Special books, or book excerpts, can also be created to fit specific needs.

For details, write: Special Markets, Alpha Books, 375 Hudson Street, New York, NY 10014.

Publisher: *Marie Butler-Knight*
Editorial Director: *Mike Sanders*
Senior Managing Editor: *Billy Fields*
Acquisitions Editor: *Michele Wells*
Development Editor: *Nancy Lewis*
Production Editor: *Kayla Dugger*

Copy Editor: *Amy Lepore*
Cartoonist: *Steve Barr*
Cover Designer: *Rebecca Harmon*
Book Designer: *Trina Wurst*
Indexer: *Tonya Heard*
Layout: *Chad Dressler*
Proofreader: *John Etchison*

Contents at a Glance

Contents

Appendixes

Foreword

In keeping with the spirit of satire implied by the word "idiot," National Master William Aramil produces a wonderfully readable chess book here. While the game of chess has a reputation of being played by rocket scientists and such, the truth is that people of all backgrounds excel at the royal game all around the world. Time-tested chess principles are passed down through the generations, and by writing a book to train the novice, William takes on a truly worthy task. Every world champion has, at some point, been a novice!

NM William Aramil himself made it to the top of the chess community for his moment in time when he won first place in the Denker Tournament of High School Champions in 2003. The American chess scene has become a truly international mix of players from around the world, particularly with many Russian Grandmasters and their offspring living and competing in America. The point is that, in attaining first place in the national event, William won not only a university scholarship but a place in history along with every yearly winner who plays in honor of the late, great Grandmaster Arnold Denker. One could go on to find other accomplishments in William's young career, but another point here is the matter of style.

Few people not well acquainted with chess realize that chess can bring regional and cultural style along with it. Perhaps few people are aware of the superb chess legacies of strong players from the Philippines or their fresh attacking style! William, being of Filipino-American descent, is no exception, and his attacking prowess and accurate board vision make him a powerful enemy at the chessboard, no matter what skill level the opponent. I have vivid memories of losing two important blitz (5-minute) games in an official event in Las Vegas to the young chess wunderkind, much to my disappointment. Along with a slashing, attacking style of his own, William has a strong grip on all phases of the game, including defensive techniques. He has much to teach as a chess trainer and, now, an author. This work will take the reader on a journey from beginner to intermediate, and the lessons taught here will continue to apply for a lifetime. Experienced players also would do well to read the book, and it is clear that the principles and variations contained herein apply equally to all who play chess.

One of the many wonderful things about the royal game is its applicability to real life and decision-making. How many times have you heard the phrase, "Life is a chess game"? Young and old will learn time-tested lessons in the dance of the lively pieces, as mate is delivered or parried in cut-and-thrust battle. Slow positional ideas will reveal themselves as maneuvers unfold across the chessboard, shaped by clear thinking. With a strong background into the workings of chess, the goddess of chess Caissa herself will smile as the novice becomes the dangerous intermediate player. Perhaps future Grandmasters will one day look back at such auspicious beginnings as offered by this book. Either way, the game and its inherent beauty and knowledge will march forward into human generations until Father Time himself adjourns the game.

—International Master Emory Andrew Tate Jr.

Emory Andrew Tate Jr. is a world-renowned chess player and linguist still active on the difficult chess circuit. Six-time Indiana State Champion and five-time Armed Forces Champion of the United States, Tate incorporates an inimitable tactical style with a deep understanding of chess principles. Emory played a small but important role in training William Aramil as a youth and takes pleasure in William's current successes, both on and away from the chessboard.

Introduction

You understand the rules of chess and can identify a checkmate, but you never seem to get out of the opening unscathed. You have always wanted to know why a Grandmaster or World Champion played a certain move in the opening, but you were never given an explanation of the idea. You often wonder, "Why doesn't the master play this move?" or "What's wrong with this idea?"

If you would like to know more about any of these areas, then this is the book for you.

Why are openings so useful to know? As with almost any aspect of life, a bad beginning or first impression can be detrimental to you—and very difficult to reverse. In a game of chess, it is essential to start with accuracy, or you may find yourself in deep waters. Taking this idea to an extreme, it is possible to lose a game of chess in two moves! (I have seen this position occur in a real game.)

Although certain players realize the significance of openings, unfortunately, some feel that it is necessary to memorize countless variations of openings to gain a quick advantage or avoid a quick loss. The main problem these players will encounter is that they lack the knowledge of the intricacies of each move and its resulting position. Chess is simply too vast to attempt to remember every possible variation within the opening. After all, there are approximately 169 octillion different combinations of positions within the first 10 moves!

I have found that the common thread to chess improvement is the assimilation of the elements of the game and the concepts of the moves played, not rote memorization. Therefore, in this guide, you will be shown the elements and ideas behind the opening moves. Hopefully, this work will provide a path to your enhancement, not only in the opening but in your entire chess game.

How This Book Is Organized

This book is presented in four sections:

Part 1, "Chess Opening Fundamentals," starts you off with the board and coordinates so that you can understand chess notation. Then

I will teach you notation so that you will be equipped to read chess moves and be able to record your own games. After that, we will take a look at the elements to help guide you through the beginning of a game. Finally, we will apply these elements to arguably the most known chess game. Part 1 is the foundation for the rest of the book, so I advise you to learn these concepts well. It will only save you time in the long run!

Part 2, "1)e4 Openings," is about the main positions that can occur after this first move from White. This is White's most popular move, and as a result, many ideas have been tested. There are some prescribed routes for White and Black to take, and we will use the elements to aid us in deciding moves that will help reach a playable position from either side of these openings.

Part 3, "1)d4 Openings," will give you insight into the more well-known positions that arise from this first move from White. Though this move follows the elements in a very similar fashion to 1)e4, White's 1)d4 usually ends up in more closed positions. That means the ideas that are used by both colors are sometimes less apparent in using the elements. A deeper look will help you to realize the truth behind moves to reach a suitable position.

Part 4, "Opening Choices," will guide you through the difficult decision of actually picking an opening to play. There is an abundance of openings, but here you will learn to use only those that have a good reputation. Then you will be equipped with the knowledge and confidence to play openings.

Things to Help You Out Along the Way

You will notice that throughout the chapters there are some special messages along the way.

Chess Language _____

In any chess book, there are many foreign words that you are bound to come across. In these notes, you will find the explanations for chess vocabulary or lingo.

The Chess Sage

In this area, I will offer general advice and give specific variations or moves.

Watch Out!

These will be warnings or pitfalls to avoid. Many times, this will be an opening trap to be aware of or rules of thumb to sidestep potential drawbacks within the game.

Acknowledgments

Thanks to the acquisitions editor, Michele Wells, for giving me the opportunity to write my first book.

Thanks to my team of editors for their suggestions and patience with me throughout this process. Also, I would like to express my gratitude to my friends: William Blackman, Isaac Braswell, David Franklin, Alex Hall, Carlton Little, Gene Scott, and Emory Tate for their help with various tasks with the book.

I am extremely thankful to Herbert Ferguson, who introduced me to my first chess tournament.

Above all, I thank my dad, Ricardo Aramil, for his years of encouragement in all of my chess endeavors. I would not have made it this far without his support in every facet of my life.

Special Thanks to the Technical Reviewer

The Complete Idiot's Guide to Chess Openings was reviewed by an expert who double-checked the accuracy and appropriateness of what you'll find here. Special thanks are extended to Mitchell Stern.

Mitchell Stern began playing chess as a high school freshman in 2001. He quickly excelled at the game, becoming one of the top high school players in New Jersey. He became the 11th Grade Champion of New Jersey in 2003, and in 2005 led his high school team to a second-place finish at the New Jersey High School Championships. Mitchell will graduate from the University of Pennsylvania in 2009 with a degree in Economics and Hispanic Studies.

Trademarks

All terms mentioned in this book that are known to be or are suspected of being trademarks or service marks have been appropriately capitalized. Alpha Books and Penguin Group (USA) Inc. cannot attest to the accuracy of this information. Use of a term in this book should not be regarded as affecting the validity of any trademark or service mark.

Part 1

Chess Opening Fundamentals

The beginning of a chess game is full of an unimaginable number of possibilities. For an inexperienced player, navigating through this maze can be an overwhelming process. Don't worry, I will simplify the subject and break down the basics. First, you will have to understand the chessboard and notation, a brief history of openings, and the overall objectives within the opening. Then I will teach you the five basic elements essential to one's success in the initial phase of a game. Finally, you will see how to apply these elements, and you can get a feel for the lasting effects these elements can have for the remainder of a chess game.

BE CAREFUL, HONEY... HIS OPENING LOOKS LIKE A TRAP!

BARR

Chapter 1

For Openers ...

In This Chapter

- ◆ The chessboard and notation
- ◆ The opening
- ◆ The history of opening names
- ◆ Objectives in the opening

Unseasoned chess players are constantly stuck or baffled by how to start a chess game. Where does one begin? It is always useful to study the basics before jumping straight into a chess game. Chess is quite vast, but if a logical approach is taken, starting off a chess game should be much easier to do. You will truly learn the chessboard and its contents to make learning chess more fun and understandable. So take a deep breath and relax. Now let's begin!

A Chess Player's Tool

From absolute beginner to Grandmaster, we must all use a chessboard. It is the universal tool to play a game of chess. I recommend memorizing the chessboard and its squares to get a better feel for the chessboard. First and foremost, you will find the information in this book much easier to absorb if you know the layout of the board.

By picturing a position in your head, you can begin to move the pieces on the board within your mind. I do not expect you to be able to make several moves in your mind at this point. With practice and patience, you will be able to imagine the board and its contents much easier. I can't promise you will be the next world chess champion, but by exercising chess "vision," you will find understanding and learning chess much simpler.

The Coordinates

How can we identify each square? Typically, a chessboard will include letters a through h running horizontally across the bottom of the board. In addition, the numbers 1 through 8 are placed vertically on the left side. This can be seen in Diagram 1.1.

Diagram 1.1: Chessboard and coordinates.

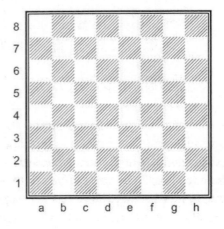

Diagram 1.1 is presented from White's point of view. It can be helpful to be able to see the position from both perspectives, but to avoid confusion I will present each diagram from White's perspective. In Diagram 1.1, every square can be named, leaving no guesswork. Essentially, the point where the letter and number cross or intersect is the name of that square. Also, when naming a square, it is proper to

write the letter first and then the number. For example, a1 refers to the square located in the bottom left-hand corner. Another possible square to look at is a8, located in the top left-hand corner.

Files, Ranks, and Diagonals

All of the squares starting with the letter a (a1–a8) are known to be on the same file. More specifically, these squares are called the a-file. There are a total of eight files, each starting with the letters a through h. Rooks and queens are the only pieces that can control an entire file. In Diagram 1.2, the a-file is clearly marked.

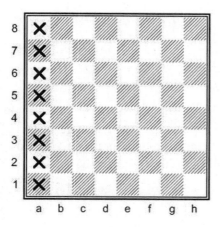

Diagram 1.2: The a-file is highlighted.

The counterpart of a file is a rank (seen in Diagram 1.3). A rank refers to the squares that are on the same row. Additionally, the squares should all end with the same number. The first rank would be the squares ending with the number 1: a1, b1, c1, d1, e1, f1, g1, and h1. There are eight total ranks: first through eighth. As you would guess, rooks and queens are the only pieces that can control a whole rank.

Another group of squares to consider is a diagonal—the squares of the same color on the same line (Diagram 1.4). The dark squares a1 through h8 (a1, b2, c3, d4, e5, f6, g7, and h8) are all part of the same diagonal. This diagonal spans the distance of the board and can be referred to as a long diagonal. Can you find all 26 diagonals in Diagram 1.4?

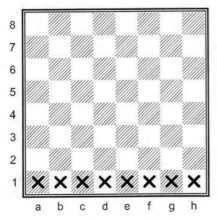

Diagram 1.3: The first rank is high-lighted.

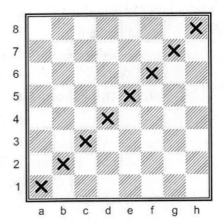

Diagram 1.4: The a1–h8 diagonal is highlighted.

Notation

You should now have a better feel for the board and some common terms. Overall, chess notation allows us to record our moves and play through chess games. I will introduce algebraic notation, the most common form of chess notation today. Here are the basics.

Name That Square

There are three main steps to write down for each and every move when using algebraic notation.

1. Use an abbreviation for the piece being moved and for pawns only when making captures. Pawn captures are typically abbreviated by the file it is on.

    Bishop = B   Queen = Q

    Knight = N   King = K

    Rook = R

2. If you are making a capture, indicate this with an (x). When the pawn captures a piece, it is abbreviated by the file (a–h) it is on. Then the (x) will follow. If no capture is made, no (x) is necessary.

3. Write the square the piece lands on.

Take a look at Diagram 1.5. Can you figure out how to write the name of that move?

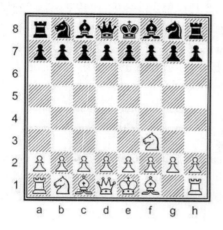

Diagram 1.5: Position after 1)Nf3.

In Diagram 1.5, White brings the knight to f3 on the first move of the game. This would be notated as Nf3. Here, the knight (N) is moved to the f3 square. Since it is White's first move of the game, it would be written as 1)Nf3. For the purpose of notation, the move numbers are important for keeping track of the order, but they do not tell you which piece has moved.

A possible response to 1)Nf3 would be 1)...e5 (Diagram 1.6).

Diagram 1.6: Position after 1)...e5.

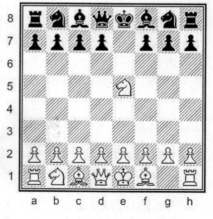

Diagram 1.7: Position after 2)Nxe5.

In Diagram 1.6, Black pushes the pawn up to the square e5. This would be notated as 1)...e5 (not a good move). Remember, it is understood that it must be a pawn move if there is no capital letter before e5 (the square the piece lands on).

White's move in Diagram 1.7 would be written as 2)Nxe5. This is White's second move of the game. So White moves the knight (N) and captures (x) the pawn on the e5 square.

Move Numbers

The move numbers for a chess game are regularly presented in two ways. First, they can be written in columns. White's moves are always in the left column, and Black's are always in the right. For example, Black's first move is e5.

1)e4	e5
2)Bc4	Nc6
3)Qh5	Nf6
4)Qxf7	#

Moves can also be notated as part of the text. This game can be expressed as 1)e4 e5 2)Bc4 Nc6 3)Qh5 Nf6 4)Qxf7 checkmate. Here, White's second move is Bc4. In some cases, this can be broken up throughout the text, only given one move at a time. The game could start off 1)e4 (commentary follows). Then the next move is 1)...e5 (more commentary). The ellipsis (...) means it is a move by Black. So, that means 1)...e5 would be Black's first move. Finally, notice that checkmate can be represented by the (#) symbol.

This or That

There are some positions where pieces such as two of White's knights can go to the same square. It must be very clear which knight has been moved. Let's take a look at a few situations. In Diagram 1.8, either of Black's knights can go to d7. Simply saying Nd7 does not tell you which of the knights goes to that square.

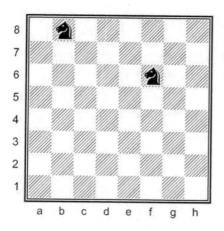

Diagram 1.8: Both Black knights can go to d7, but how are they notated?

The best way to avoid the confusion is to refer to the file or rank the piece is on. If you were to move the knight on b8 to d7, it would be written as Nbd7 (Diagram 1.9). If we break down each letter within Nbd7, we would have an (N) for the knight being moved, (b) for the file the knight is on, and d7, the destination of the knight. How would you write the other knight on f6 going to d7? First, (N) to represent the knight, (f) to say it is on the f-file, and d7 for the square where it ends up. Put it together and it is written as Nfd7.

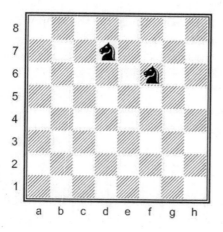

Diagram 1.9: Position after Nbd7.

If both pieces that can move to the same square are also on the same file, then you can show the difference by using the rank of the piece. You might be thinking, "What if they are on the same file and rank?" Well, it is impossible because that would mean two pieces would have to be on the same square. The rules and squares on a chessboard permit only one piece per square.

Writing Special Moves

There are only two ways to notate *castling*, and they depend on what side you have castled. If you castle the shorter way, or on the *kingside*, it would be written as 0-0 (Diagram 1.10). If you castle on the long side, or *queenside*, it is written as 0-0-0 (Diagram 1.11).

Chess Language _____

Castling is a special move involving both a rook and the king. The king moves two squares in the direction of a rook and the rook transfers to the other side directly next to the king. Once the king or rook has moved, castling is no longer allowed with that piece. Also, you cannot castle while in check or if either of the squares that the king passes through are controlled by any of the opponent's pieces.

The chessboard can be split in half: a- through d-files and e- through h-files. The **kingside** is known as all the squares on the e-, f-, g-, and h-files. The **queenside** is all the squares located on the a- through d-files.

The rules for writing *en passant* follow the three-step process. Don't get thrown off by the fact that you take an opponent's pawn but end up on a different square. Remember, the square your pawn goes to is the square you would write. You will also sometimes see the abbreviation e.p. (en passant) after the notated move.

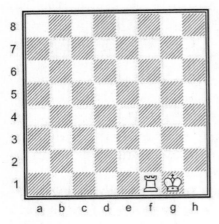

Diagram 1.10: Position after White castles kingside.

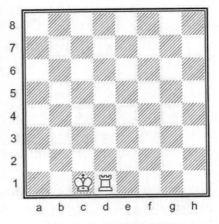

Diagram 1.11: Position after White castles queenside.

Chess Language

The phrase **en passant** is French for "in passing." As a pawn moves from its original square two spaces and is side by side an opponent's pawn, an en passant can be done. Once the pawn moves two squares, the opponent's pawn can capture that pawn as if it had only moved one square. Also, when the pawn moves two squares from its original position, an en passant must be done immediately. You cannot let one move pass, or it will be against the rules to perform this special move.

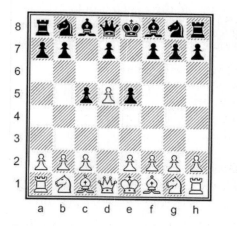

Diagram 1.12: Position after 1)d4 c5 2)d5 e5.

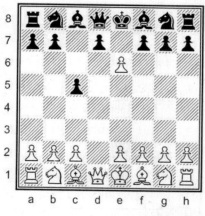

Diagram 1.13: Position after 3)dxe6 e.p.

The position in Diagram 1.12 is a result of the moves 1)d4 c5 2)d5 e5. In Diagram 1.12, Black has just played 2)...e5. White can perform an en passant by playing 3)dxe6 e.p. (Diagram 1.13). Although the Black pawn is on e5, the White pawn cannot go to that square. You can't say dxe5 because your pawn does not go to that square, and pawns are not allowed to capture sideways. According to the rules of chess, pawns only capture in diagonals, even when executing an en passant. Therefore, you write the move as if you were capturing a pawn on e6. Since the pawn ends up on e6, it is written as dxe6 e.p. The (d) is for the file the pawn is on, (x) is for the capture, and e6 tells you the destination of the pawn. The e.p. lets the reader know it was an en passant and not an impossible move.

Chess Language

In chess, to **promote** simply means to turn the pawn into a piece of a higher value. Since the queen holds the highest value, promoting the pawn into a queen is usually the best option. This is not always the case, but that is the beauty of chess: there are always exceptions.

Then add the abbreviation e.p. When a pawn reaches the other side of the board, it may *promote* into a knight, bishop, rook, or queen. This means that it is important to say what piece the pawn will become. Let's say you had a pawn on d7, and you pushed it to d8 turning the pawn into a queen. This would be expressed as d8Q. Just remember, follow the three-step process, then add the abbreviation of the piece you would like to promote the pawn into.

As a reminder, here is the three-step process for notation:

1. Use an abbreviation for the piece being moved and for pawns only when making captures.

2. If you are making a capture, indicate this with an (x).

3. Write the square that piece lands on.

Symbols

We have covered the main ideas, but there are some additional symbols to know when reading annotations. Sometimes there will be a symbol such as an exclamation point or a question mark after a notated move.

The following are common symbols you might encounter in this book:

+	Check
++	Double check
#	Checkmate
!	Good move
!!	Brilliant move
?	Bad move
??	Blunder

!?	Interesting move
?!	Dubious move
1-0	White wins
$\frac{1}{2}$-$\frac{1}{2}$	Draw
0-1	Black wins

These symbols always follow the notated move.

An example game is as follows:

1)f3	e5
2)g4??	Qh4# 0-1

In Diagram 1.14, Black's second move was queen to h4. Additionally, the 0-1 means Black has won, and it comes after the (#) symbol. You should only see two symbols in a row if the game has come to an end. Okay, I know that can be a lot. If you take notation step-by-step, you will find the whole process less complicated. As you read more chess notation, eventually it will become second nature.

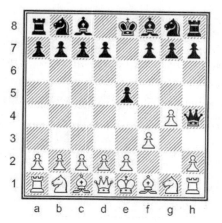

Diagram 1.14: Position after 2)...Qh4# 0-1.

The Opening vs. an Opening?

From beginning to end, a chess game is known to consist of three stages: the opening, *middlegame*, and *endgame*. The opening refers to the initial series of moves, generally lasting the first 10 moves. There

Chess Language

The **middlegame** in chess refers to the stage that comes directly after the opening. Strategic and tactical maneuvers for attacking and defending take place in this part of the game. When the queens have been traded or very few pieces remain on the board, then the **endgame** begins. Once a piece moves from its starting position, it means it has been **developed**.

is no rule saying when the opening must end, but it is considered to be finished when the majority of pieces have been *developed*, and both sides have castled.

Every opening begins with the same starting position (Diagram 1.15). Not to be confused with *the* opening, *an* opening is a specific series of moves recognizable by a set formation of the pieces. An identifiable opening can be seen in Diagram 1.16. This formation is called the Ruy Lopez.

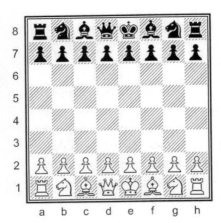

Diagram 1.15: The starting position.

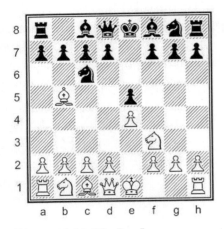

Diagram 1.16: The Ruy Lopez.

Opening Names

Chess openings have most commonly adopted their names from chess players themselves. In some cases, they have been named after countries or nationalities. Rarely are they descriptions of positions or named after animals. A very popular opening is called the Sicilian Defense (Diagram 1.17). Not only does this contain a nationality (Sicilian), it is telling you the idea (defense—which is typically Black's first move in response to White's first move).

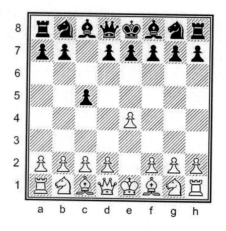

Diagram 1.17: The Sicilian Defense.

Usually, there are two words to explain the origin (Sicilian) and the idea (defense) of an opening. The Sicilian Defense is fairly accurate, but other openings may be misnamed.

A Good Beginning

As with almost any aspect of life, a bad start or first impression can be detrimental and very difficult to reverse. In the opening of a chess game, it is imperative to move with accuracy, or you may find yourself in deep waters. If you would like to avoid a quick loss or possibly gain an advantage, knowledge of openings is a high priority. For example, in Diagram 1.14, White gets checkmated in two moves because of little opening knowledge. This bears the notorious name of Fool's Mate.

The Goal

If I were to sum up the idea of openings with one word, it would be mobilization. In terms of war, this refers to preparing yourself for battle. This is where you gather the necessary equipment and place your soldiers in the most effective positions. In a chess game, you can use the same reasoning. With the White or Black pieces, your goal should be to bring out as many pieces as possible from their starting squares. Since you are the

Chess Language

A **playable position** is a relatively balanced position, with chances for both sides. Ultimately, if you have reached a playable position, winning is a definite possibility.

general, it is your job to figure out what pieces belong where. You will not necessarily use all of your pieces in the beginning. These unused pieces can be your so-called reserves, just in case you need them. By mobilizing your pieces, your basic purpose is to reach at least a *playable position*. These are very general ideas, but you will see more specific ideas in the next two chapters.

The Least You Need to Know

- ◆ Memorize the chessboard and squares—the building blocks for learning chess.
- ◆ Mastering notation is your first step to reading chess moves.
- ◆ A poor start or opening can spell doom for your game.
- ◆ Mobilization is the first step to a good opening.

2

Basic Elements of Chess Openings

In This Chapter

- ◆ Too many possibilities to memorize
- ◆ The five elements
- ◆ King safety takes precedence

The opening stage of a game contains near-limitless possibilities. Therefore, it is only logical to apply elements or principles within not only the opening but the entire game. Within just the general 10-move boundary of openings, there are approximately 169 octillion possible positions. For those whose busy schedules will not permit them to look up the word octillion, well … 169,000,000,000,000,000,000,000,000,000.

If you did not decipher the meaning of octillion, it is a 1 followed by 27 zeros! Incredible! This is far beyond the capacity of any normal human. That's why I will teach you openings from a logical approach based on five elements: material, time, space, pawn structure, and king safety. You will have an inside look at the effects each element will have on a position. Then you will be equipped to put these elements to use.

Material

Each piece has an estimated point or relative value. They are given these values because of their power (the number of squares each piece can attack or move to).

- ◆ Pawn = 1
- ◆ Knight = 3
- ◆ Bishop = 3

- ◆ Rook = 5
- ◆ Queen = 9
- ◆ King = Game

In many cases, you can use this point system as a guideline. For instance, according to these values, you would never want to trade a queen (9 points) for your opponent's knight (3 points). However, what if a piece has been immobilized and has no available squares? That means its value has diminished. For the most part, each piece is only as good as its possible squares.

Time

Stop looking at your watch! I do not mean that type of time. When players speak of time in chess, they are mostly referring to the speed at which you develop your pieces. Here are some ways to gain time in a chess game:

1. Try to develop as many different *minor pieces* toward the *center* of the board.

2. Maximize the scope of each piece. The more squares a piece controls, the larger purpose it is likely serving.

3. Avoid moving the same piece twice unless necessary or advantageous.

4. Create threats such as material, thus forcing your opponent to waste time in response.

5. Avoid developing your pieces to squares that allow your opponent to threaten them and thereby gain a *tempo*.

Chess Language _____

A **minor piece** is a knight or bishop. It should be a priority to activate minor pieces instead of rooks and the queen in the opening.

The **center** is considered the squares in the middle of the board: d4, d5, e4, and e5. A **tempo** is another word for a turn or move. By gaining a tempo, you can obtain an extra or free move. The plural of tempo is tempi.

Space

Space is another word for territory and refers to the total number of squares one controls on the chessboard. With respect to wars, having more space tends to secure some strategic advantage. If you are a general with many soldiers, it makes no sense to have them bunched together stepping on each other's toes. These fighters will find it easier to spread out in battle without interfering with each other's strikes ... and, of course, their toes.

Seizing Squares

To gain real space, you must control squares with your pieces on your opponent's half of the board. Think about this: if your pieces never cross the demarcation line (the imaginary line separating the board in half), how can you win? It can happen, but it is not likely. If you are White, all possible squares that any of your pieces can move to between the fifth and eighth rank is the space you truly control. This idea is illustrated in Diagram 2.1.

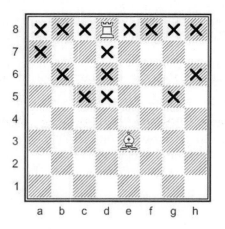

Diagram 2.1: The highlighted squares are the true space the pieces control.

The White rook controls space on d5, d6, d7, and the entire eighth rank. The White bishop controls a7, b6, c5, g5, and h6. Despite the other squares the rook and bishop can move to, they are not considered space that they control.

Nevertheless, you can help your space by preventing your opponent from controlling squares on your half of the board.

From the very start, it is wise to gain space. The most common way to achieve more space is through the center. For more space, place your pawns in the center of the board and develop pieces around those central squares. The main objective is to move your minor pieces and pawns to squares that allow you to control the most number of squares on your opponent's half of the board. Essentially, the center and space go hand in hand. Also, do not move your pieces to vulnerable squares where they can be easily attacked (the threat of losing material) or pushed back, losing ground.

The Chess Sage

Almost every great Grandmaster believes that centralization is the key idea to fight for space. When your pieces are in the center, they are mobile and have more options. If a piece is on the side of the board (a- or h-file), it cannot go both left and right. Fight for the center, not the side!

I Have Space and ...

When your pieces control more squares, they have more power. This is the best time to go after your opponent's king or attack the main weakness of your opponent's position. If this can't be done immediately, grab more space to make it more difficult for your opponent to mobilize his or her pieces. Space by itself does not mean anything unless you can gain something else. Don't just sit on your advantage; be aggressive.

When a space advantage is obtained, the following rule is repeated: "Avoid trading pieces." One may know the rule, but you must truly understand the position on the chessboard. If your pieces are controlling many squares, it hardly makes sense to trade these pieces. Basically, "avoid trading pieces" of yours that are dominating the chessboard. Take a look at Diagram 2.2 to understand this idea. White could take the bishop on c8 with the knight, but that would be a waste. The knight on d6 is assertively controlling squares in Black's camp, but the bishop on c8 does not even control one square on the board. Although the knight and bishop are equal in value, the knight has a greater presence in the game. Don't trade such powerful pieces!

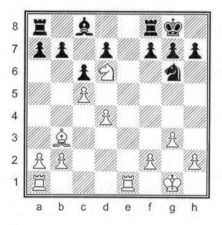

Diagram 2.2: Should White trade the knight on d6 for Black's bishop on c8?

Help, I Can't Breathe

To a Grandmaster of chess, having little space or lack thereof is comparable to having no air. The absence of space in the opening can have suffocating effects for the remainder of the game. When rapidly losing air, don't panic. If you move around aimlessly, you will run out of air even quicker. Although your position may require some CPR, there is still time to develop a meaningful plan. If you feel that your space is inadequate, here are some life-saving principles to guide you:

1. Remove or trade pieces that are cramping your position.

2. Use lesser-valued pieces such as pawns to force back more powerful pieces stopping your progress.

3. Try to create a counterattack at your opponent's weakest point.

4. If possible, attack your opponent's space advantage head on.

Pawn Structure

Imagine two opposing armies on a direct collision course. The soldiers in front must bear the brunt of the initial contact. These are the pawns.

You are the general who will determine the strategy and formation of these frontline soldiers. Where you decide to place these pawns will determine your pawn structure on the chessboard.

Essentially, the organization and placement of your pawns is pawn structure. Although the pawns are modest in size and value, other pieces, except the knights, cannot join the battle unless the pawns are moved.

The Soul of Chess

As André Danican Philidor once said, "Pawns are the soul of chess." Although, according to the relative value of the pieces, pawns are the least valuable. Then why are they so important? Pawns outnumber any other piece on the board, and they are critical in determining the style of the game. When a pawn attacks a more valuable piece, it should move away to avoid the loss of material. Likewise, a more valuable piece such as a knight would typically not go to a square where it could be captured by a pawn. Pawns establish the style, pace, and structure of the opening. Your pawns can have lasting effects for the rest of the game.

The Chess Sage

Pawn moves are extremely committal because, once moved, they can't move backward. It will be useful to know how to handle their deficiencies and prosper from their strengths.

Pawn Chains

These are a sequence of pawns located on the same diagonal. The pawn that is least advanced is referred to as the base. Both White and Black have pawn chains in Diagram 2.3.

In Diagram 2.3, White's pawn chain consists of the pawns on b2, c3, d4, and e5. Black's pawn chain includes the pawns on c4, d5, e6, and f7. Pawn chains can be very useful in cutting off your opponent's pieces and hindering mobility. Meanwhile, you can form an attack while your opponent is trying to break through the wall.

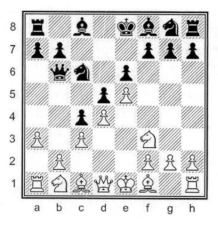

Diagram 2.3: Pawn chains.

Pawn Islands

All the pawns you begin a game with are part of a society. Once a pawn or group of pawns breaks off from this society, it is considered a pawn island. There may be multiple islands or societies formed when the pawns break off from the initial society. More specifically, a pawn island is a single pawn or group of pawns of the same color. Moreover, to be considered a pawn island, there cannot be any pawns of the same color on the adjacent files. In Diagram 2.4, White has three pawn islands: (a2 and b2), (d4), and (f2, g2, and h2). Black has only two pawn islands: (a7, b7, and c6) and (f7, g7, and h7).

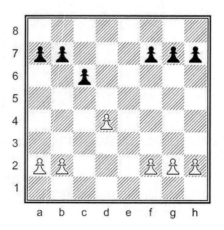

Diagram 2.4: Pawn islands.

Watch Out! _____

Avoid creating too many pawn islands! Your pawns work as a cohesive unit. If multiple pawn islands are created, they can be attacked much easier. Just as in most scary movies, one group will break up into many pairs, but eventually these pairs are picked off one by one. Don't fall victim to the same fate!

Isolated Pawn

This is a more specific type of pawn island. This refers to a single pawn with no pawns of the same color on the files next to it. In Diagram 2.5, the pawn on d4 is an example of an isolated pawn. More often than not, isolated pawns are weaknesses in one's position. The reason is that it is impossible for a teammate to protect an isolated pawn. In Diagram 2.5, the bishop on f6 attacks the pawn on d4, but White has no effective way of protecting the pawn.

Take a look at the difference if this White pawn on d4 were not isolated. In Diagram 2.6, White can play c3, and it is no longer wise for Black to capture the pawn on d4.

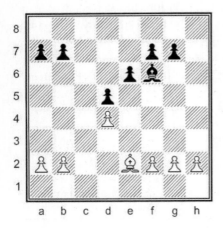

Diagram 2.5: White's pawn on d4 is isolated and cannot be saved.

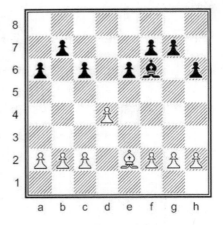

Diagram 2.6: White can play c3 to protect the pawn on d4 now.

Backward Pawn

Can you picture soldiers marching, each one standing behind the other and ready to protect his comrades? There is one lingering problem—who is supposed to protect the last man? No one is standing behind the last man, leaving him most vulnerable. When a pawn has no compatriot for support, it is considered backward. Additionally, the pawn cannot move forward without being exposed to a capture. This means the square in front of the pawn can be used by the opponent as a post at his or her leisure. The pawn on e3 in Diagram 2.7 is considered a backward pawn. It cannot be protected by another pawn, and if it moves forward, it will be wiped out from existence.

Diagram 2.7: White's pawn on e3 is a backward pawn.

Two Many

One idea is to shy away from having two pawns of the same color on the same file. These are called doubled pawns. Doubled pawns can interfere with one another, and they can't defend one another. Too many pawns on the same file can be redundant and a waste of man-power. In Diagram 2.8, the limitations of doubled pawns can be seen.

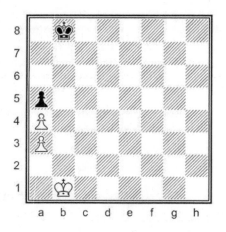

Diagram 2.8: White has an extra pawn, but since the two pawns are doubled, the game is a theoretically drawn position.

King Safety: The Trump Card

When all is said and done, there is only one objective: to checkmate your opponent's king. You must never forget about king safety. So far, we have discussed the significance of material, time, space, and pawn structure in the opening and the lasting effects they may have in the game. In spite of the importance of these principles, king safety trumps them all. After all, if your own king has been checkmated, it doesn't matter how much material you have or how pretty your pawn structure looks!

The best way to provide a safe home for your king is to castle. Another key reason for using this maneuver is to bring a rook into the game. The rook is worth approximately 5 points, so it is important to use this piece for open files and preparing for an attack in the middlegame. When few pieces remain, rooks are also useful in the endgame. The game starting with Diagram 2.9 will reveal the great importance of castling.

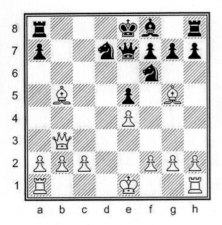

Diagram 2.9: Paul Morphy vs. Duke Karl and his assistant Count Isouard.

Diagram 2.10: Position after 12)0-0-0.

Diagram 2.9 is an extremely famous position. It is a game between Paul Morphy (White) and Duke Karl of Brunswick/Count Isouard of Paris (Black), who partnered up to increase their chances against the legendary Morphy. Here, White has given up a piece for two pawns, leaving

Morphy down a net of one point. However, because of the poor king position of Black, White has a winning position. Morphy played the perfectly timed 12)0-0-0 (Diagram 2.10). Here White's move serves two purposes. He tucks his king behind his pawns, preventing 12)...Qb4+. (Black wants to trade queens and weaken White's attack.) He also brings the rook on a1 into the game, allowing it to control space on the d-file.

What can Black do? White has the immediate threat of Bxd7+, or even Rxd7, and Black would lose material. So Black is essentially forced to play 12)...Rd8 to defend (Diagram 2.11). If 12) ... 0-0-0, Black will have to surrender after 13)Ba6+Kc7 14)Qb7#.

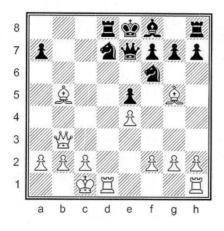

Diagram 2.11: Position after 12)...Rd8.

In Diagram 2.11, White has all of his pieces primed and ready for a full assault. The White side has a large space advantage, but it will only prove beneficial if White can find the breakthrough in the position. I have shown this position to students, and they have most frequently recommended 13)Rd2. The idea is to play Rhd1 to double the rooks on the d-file. This is still a good move, but it will give Black a small chance to save the game. For example, after Black's move 13)...Qb4, a sample variation runs 14)Rhd1 Qxb3 15)axb3 Bc5 16)Bxf6 gxf6 17)Rxd7 0-0 19)f3. This position leaves White up two pawns, but White will still have to demonstrate a little technique to win. White should strive for more, which is exactly what Morphy did. Let us refer back to Diagram 2.11. Morphy played the stunning 13)Rxd7 seen in Diagram 2.12! Black is forced to play 13)...Rxd7 to avoid material loss (Diagram 2.13).

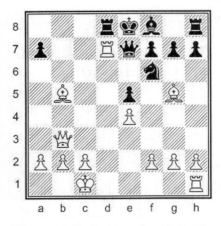

Diagram 2.12: Position after 13)Rxd7.

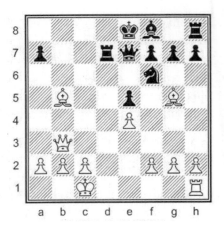

Diagram 2.13: Position after 13)... Rxd7.

Before Black can escape the vice grip, White must add more pressure with 14)Rd1 (Diagram 2.14). The White queen controls a lot of space, and this can only be dangerous for the Black king. Black thinks he can escape the attack by trading queens and reducing White's space advantage. This is the right idea, but Black has taken too much time, and some pieces have yet to be developed. For this reason, Black is losing the game despite being ahead in material. So in Diagram 2.15, the Duke/Count played 14)...Qe6. After 14)...Qe6, White plays 15)Bxd7+ in Diagram 2.16. What was Morphy's idea behind capturing the rook? Now Black is relatively forced to play 15)...Nxd7 (Diagram 2.17).

Diagram 2.14: Position after 14)Rd1.

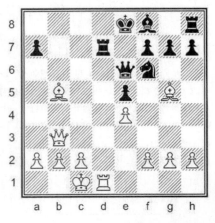

Diagram 2.15: Position after 14)...Qe6.

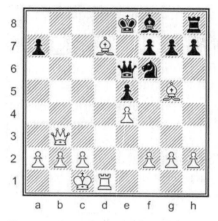

Diagram 2.16: Position after 15)Bxd7+.

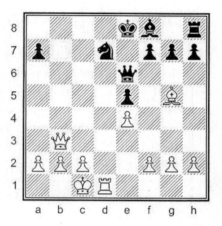

Diagram 2.17: Position after 15)… Nxd7.

It is time to assess the resulting position in Diagram 2.17. White is still down a piece for two pawns, leaving Morphy down one point. Even though Black is up a point, the king is extremely exposed. Also, while all of White's pieces have been developed, Black still has a bishop on f8 and a rook on h8 that have not been touched. The rook on h8 is especially useless as it controls no real squares. If you do not castle in the game, it can sometimes be a challenge to give the rook meaning. Black never had time to castle in the game and, as a result, will have a losing game. How did Morphy hammer in the last nail in the coffin?

The Chess Sage

We have reached the most critical position in the entire game (Diagram 2.17)! I know you can feel it, too, but the exact moves are not so obvious. I will attempt to simplify the thinking process. In any position in chess, imagine your pieces on the best squares possible. Once you have done that, you can figure out the steps to achieve the best position for your pieces.

Consider the best squares for the White pieces. Better yet, if you could place one piece anywhere on the board for White, where would you put it? This includes illegal moves. Once you correctly imagine this, the position afterward should be a checkmate. Okay, there are two right answers: you could place a queen on c8 or a rook on d8 to checkmate the king. Now, how do we actually get the queen to those squares? Refer to Diagram 2.17 for the following analysis. The best way to get the queen to c8 is via b7. What can Black do after 16)Qb7? Black has a way to escape the madness by 16)...f6. The most logical line continues with 17)Qc8+ Ke7 18)Be3 g6 19)Qc7 Ke8 20)Bxa7. This position is materially equal, but White still has a large positional advantage. At the moment, White has three pawns for a piece, and Black's king is walking a tightrope. Also, in some variations, White will win the piece back and be up three clear *passed pawns*. White is clearly better, but there are chances for White to misplay the current position. To be objective, 16)Qb7 is not the best move for White to play.

Chess Language

A **passed pawn** is a pawn that does not encounter any opponent's pawns on the same or adjacent files.

Take a look at Diagram 2.17 again. What is the best move in the position then? Remember, the other possible square to imagine was the d8 square. You would like the White rook to be on d8 because this would be a checkmate. How does the White rook get to the d8 square if the knight on d7 is blocking the passage? The first option to always ponder is the forcing variations. Is it possible to force the knight from d7? Yes! I know you can find the devastating blow that Morphy handed the two minds. Take your time. This game was immortalized by Morphy's next move, practically known by the majority of masters. Morphy plays 16)Qb8+!! (Diagram 2.18)

Diagram 2.18: Position after 16)Qb8+!!

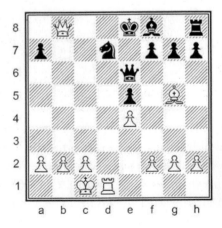

White gives up the queen to force the knight from d7 so that 17)Rd8 checkmate can be played. Morphy *sacrifices* a queen for checkmate. We tried to mimic the thought processes of Morphy, and by doing so, we came to the same answer. The aim of our thinking was to

Chess Language

A **sacrifice** means to give up material or points in hopes of gaining an advantage in one of the other elements.

remove the knight by force so that we can place the rook on d8. Black must play 16)...Nxb8 to escape the check (Diagram 2.19).

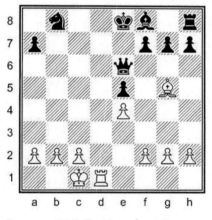

Diagram 2.19: Position after 16)... Nxb8.

Diagram 2.20: Position after 17)Rd8#.

Without further ado, Paul Morphy played 17)Rd8 checkmate (Diagram 2.20). In the final position, shown in Diagram 2.20, Black is up a total of 10 points. Black is up a queen and knight for two pawns but has been checkmated despite the advantage in material. If we try to determine where Black went wrong, the root of the problem was the weakness of the king's position. White gained more space because Black fell behind in the development of his pieces because of defending attacks. As a result, Black was never able to move the bishop on f8 to clear the space for castling. Black ran out of time. Even though White was on the prowl for the Black king, he still found time to castle. Morphy (White) solidified his own king's position and activated his rook to assure his victory.

The Least You Need to Know

◆ Chess has too many possibilities to memorize.

◆ The five elements—material, time, space, pawn structure, and king safety—can help guide you through openings.

◆ It is wise to follow principles but more meaningful to know when to apply them.

◆ Checkmate rules all!

Chapter 3

The Elements in Motion

In This Chapter

- ◆ Learning to apply principles to a game
- ◆ Putting it all together
- ◆ Deciding who has the advantage

You have seen the elements that can have a vital role in your opening play. Each element has its unique qualities, but when playing a game, they must not be viewed as separate entities. Having the benefit in one element many times can assist with the others. The five principles of material, time, space, pawn structure, and king safety should be considered one. Neglecting any of these elements can be fatal!

When one has a lead in time, it means that more pieces are active, and as a result more space is usually controlled. Since one side has more soldiers in place and more territory is gained, an attack on the enemy fort or king is very logical. Now what if, during the confrontation, part of your army is lost and scattered? The analogy to chess is that your material and pawn structure have been negotiated. The concept: if the enemy survives the initial onslaught, your endgame may very well be compromised. Of course, if the attack is successful, you win the game.

This sounds like a very complex struggle, but we will examine the famous game played by Paul Morphy once again to get a great feel of how these elements are intertwined. You will see how following the elements is used in the opening to gain a great position. From this model game, you will learn how the elements can be applied and evaluated in your own chess games.

Analyzing Opening Variations

The game that we will analyze is between Morphy (White) and Duke Karl/Count Isouard (Black). Hopefully you have read Chapter 2 and have already seen the results of the opening play starting from move 12. Now we will look at the game from move one. Morphy launches off with 1)e4 (Diagram 3.1).

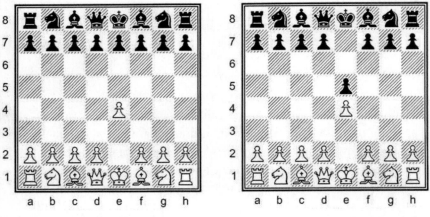

Diagram 3.1: Position after 1)e4.   Diagram 3.2: Position after 1)...e5.

Statistically speaking, 1)e4 is by far the most popular first move in the history of chess. This is no random occurrence, as this move agrees with the elements. 1)e4 grabs space in the center occupying the e4 square and controlling the d5 and f5 squares. Meanwhile, it opens up the diagonals for the bishop on f1 and the queen on d1. Even though the bishop and queen have not moved yet, they still control squares on the opponent's half of the board. The Duke and the Count play 1)...e5 (Diagram 3.2).

Historically, 1)...e5 is the most common move in response to 1)e4, although 1)...c5 is becoming more popular today. Like 1)e4, 1)...e5 is also very conscientious of the elements, and it is a useful move for identical reasons as 1)e4. It controls space and allows other pieces to join the battle.

White continues routinely with 2)Nf3, the most dominant choice of all time (Diagram 3.3). White develops the knight while attacking the e5 pawn and gaining a tempo (time). Another plus this move offers is that it helps clear the squares for a kingside castle. Black follows with 2)...d6 (Diagram 3.4). This move protects the e5 pawn, but no minor piece is developed. It does open up the diagonal for the bishop on c8, but that is canceled out because 2)...d6 limits the diagonal of the bishop on f8.

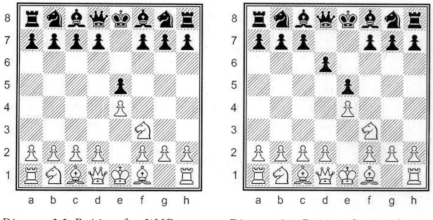

Diagram 3.3: Position after 2)Nf3.   Diagram 3.4: Position after 2)...d6.

In Diagram 3.5, White plays 3)d4, aggressively pushing the pawn to the center (space) and attacking the e5 target twice (time). Black uses the counter measure 3)...Bg4?! (Diagram 3.6). At a quick glance, it appears to be a decent move. Black develops a bishop and indirectly protects the e5 pawn by *pinning* the White knight. For Black to maintain material equality, he must surrender the bishop. The Black bishop will make its second move of the game while capturing a knight that has only moved once (time). 3)...Nf6 is a better move for Black.

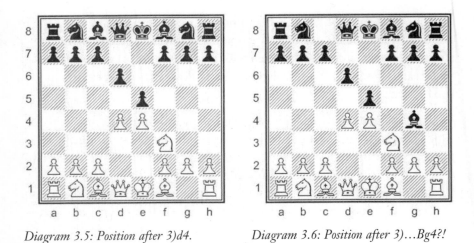

Diagram 3.5: Position after 3)d4.   *Diagram 3.6: Position after 3)...Bg4?!*

In Diagram 3.7, White continues with the correct plan 4)dxe5, forcing Black to lose a pawn or time. If Black plays the unaware 4)...dxe5, White will play 5)Qxd8+. The White knight is no longer pinned. Then Black is forced to play 5)...Kxd8, forfeiting castling. White will follow with 6)Nxe5, winning a pawn. This knight threatens the bishop on g4 as well as the f7 square *forking* the king and rook. This is a poor choice for Black. So Black plays the logical 4)...Bxf3 instead (Diagram 3.8). Black moves the bishop for a second time to capture a knight that has only moved once (time). Black also gives up the *bishop pair*, which in turn weakens the light squares.

Chess Language

To **pin** means to immobilize an opponent's valued piece. For example, in Diagram 3.6, if the knight on f3 moves, it will allow the bishop to capture the queen—losing material. A **fork** is an attack on two pieces or more. (See the definition of "double attack" later in this chapter.) The **bishop pair** refers to the side with both the light- and dark-squared bishops. Typically, when one of these bishops is lost, the squares of that colored bishop become weak. This is especially true if the opponent still has the bishop of that color.

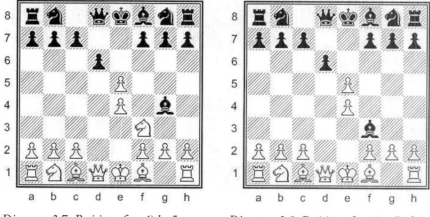

Diagram 3.7: Position after 4)dxe5.   *Diagram 3.8: Position after 4)...Bxf3.*

White correctly recaptures the bishop with 5)Qxf3 (Diagram 3.9). The other logical move would be 5)gxf3, but this creates doubled pawns (pawn structure). In Diagram 3.10, Black responds 5)...dxe5 to avoid being a pawn down (material). Now White plays a move that has many great attributes: 6)Bc4 (Diagram 3.11). First, it develops a piece. Second, checkmate is also threatened with 7)Qxf7. Finally, it frees up the last square for White to castle (time, space, and king safety).

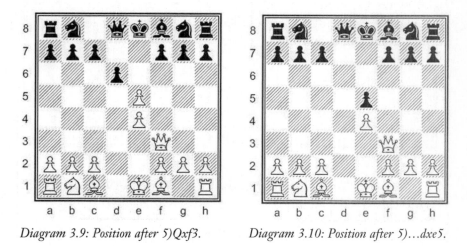

Diagram 3.9: Position after 5)Qxf3.   *Diagram 3.10: Position after 5)...dxe5.*

In Diagram 3.12, Black plays the very unassuming developing move 6)...Nf6. It stops the checkmate while developing a piece toward the center. Are there any possible flaws to this move? Morphy plays the laterally disguised 7)Qb3 (Diagram 3.13). White moves the queen for the second time in the game, but there is a good reason. The White queen attacks the pawn on b7 and also forms a *battery* with the bishop on c4 that attacks the f7 square. The White queen creates a *double attack*, threatening to win two different pawns (material). How does Black cope with the multiple threats? Black must give up the pawn on either b7 or f7.

Diagram 3.11: Position after 6)Bc4.

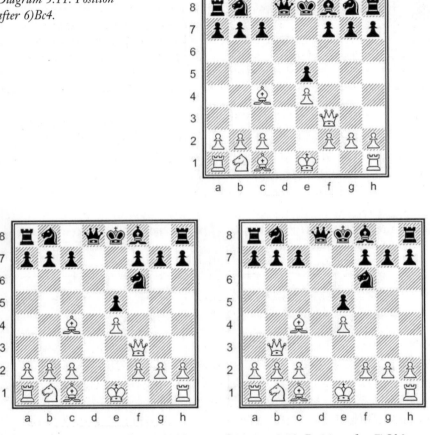

Diagram 3.12: Position after 6)...Nf6.   *Diagram 3.13: Position after 7)Qb3.*

Black must defend the pawn on f7, preventing mate in two: 8)Bxf7+ Kd7 or Ke7 9)Qe6 checkmate. Therefore, Black moves 7)...Qe7 to protect the f7 square (Diagram 3.14). The clear drawback of this move is that it blocks the bishop on f8. Another idea of 7)...Qe7 with a positive value is that after 8)Qxb7, Black will play 8)...Qb4+, forcing queen trades

9)Qxb4 Bxb4+ 10)c3. After this, White will be up a pawn (material), but since the queens are gone, the game will most likely be decided in the endgame. This would still be objectively winning, yet Morphy (White) was not going to have that ....

Chess Language _____

A **battery** is when two or more pieces (queen and bishop) help each other attack on the same file, rank, or diagonal. A **double attack** is when one piece attacks two or more different opponent pieces. A double attack can also be when two pieces attack two different opponent's pieces, as in a discovered attack.

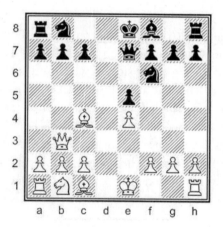

Diagram 3.14: Position after 7)...Qe7.

White plays the powerful and poised 8)Nc3 (Diagram 3.15). Wow! Morphy shows an unbelievable patience with the position. Most players would have captured the free pawn on b7. However, this would have been the third time within the first eight moves that the White queen has moved (time). So Morphy prefers to deploy another minor piece and control more space with 8)Nc3. Black is blindly grateful and plays 8)...c6 (Diagram 3.16). The idea of this move is to protect the pawn on b7 with the queen. Still, Black is not helping his cause, as he has only developed one minor piece—the knight.

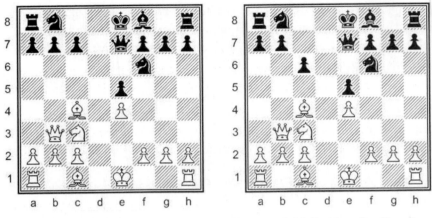

Diagram 3.15: Position after 8)Nc3.   Diagram 3.16: Position after 8)...c6.

White brings along another friend with 9)Bg5 (Diagram 3.17). This bishop pins the knight on f6 and tightens the straitjacket. It also frees up the space for White to castle on the queenside. If we closely inspect Diagram 3.17, the material and pawn structure of both sides are balanced, but White has a clear positional edge due to the other elements. White has three minor pieces developed as opposed to Black's one. Because of this lead in time and development, Morphy also controls more space. Since he has more pieces out in the open controlling more squares, he is ready to overpower his opponent. Not to be forgotten, White is also ready to castle on the very next move, while Black is three moves away.

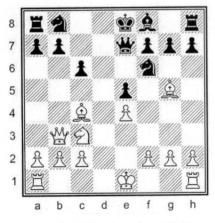

Diagram 3.17: Position after 9)Bg5.

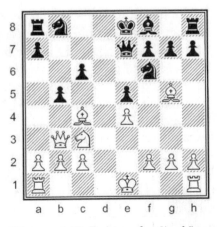

Diagram 3.18: Position after 9)...b5.

It would be ideal for Black to play 9)...Nbd7, but White would take the pawn on b7 with 10)Qxb7 free of charge. In Diagram 3.18, Black plays 9)...b5 so that the b-pawn is no longer in harm's way after Nbd7. The move 9)...b5 is also an attempt to gain a free move, forcing the bishop to retreat. Black could then try 10)...Nbd7 for a playable position.

White plays the seemingly shocking 10)Nxb5 (Diagram 3.19). To the untrained eye, this may seem to be a surprising move since it gives up material. The main idea of this sacrifice is to open up lines and avenues toward the king. To understand this position and the move played, we must apply the elements. White has a superior lead in development (time), his pieces control more squares (space), and Black's king has not castled (king safety). Despite the fact that White will lose material after 10)...cxb5, the position is as if White is up material. This means that White has more useful and active pieces in the game. All of White's minor pieces have been developed. Meanwhile, Black has not moved the knight on b8, the bishop on f8 is suffocated, and the rook on h8 is absolutely meaningless. To further add to the problems, it will take too long to activate these pieces so that Black can castle. As you will see, 10)Nxb5 is absolutely justified!

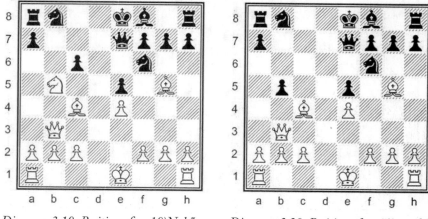

Diagram 3.19: Position after 10)Nxb5.   Diagram 3.20: Position after 10)...cxb5.

White could have also tried sacrificing the bishop by 10)Bxb5?!, but this piece needs to control the diagonal to attack the king. After Black captures the bishop (10)...cxb5), White will play 11)Nxb5. These few moves by White prove to be inaccurate because this allows Black to play 11)...Qb4+ (trading queens) and extinguish White's upper hand. Black's king will no longer be in danger, and Black will be up material.

After 10)Nxb5, Black plays the obvious capture 10)...cxb5 to gain material (Diagram 3.20). By taking the knight, he opens up a diagonal to his king while it's stuck in the middle of the board. In Chapter 2, we were able to see how this game ended, but it is not so easy to decline a sacrifice and see that far in the future. Black took the bait but should have swallowed his pride and traded queens with 10)...Qb4+ to get rid of White's dominant piece. Granted, Black would still be down at least a pawn and have many weaknesses, but he would not have lost so quickly. Maybe he knew all of this and did not want to delay the inevitable. I highly doubt it ....

White captures the pawn and attacks the king on the diagonal with 11)Bxb5+ (Diagram 3.21). Here, White puts the Black king in check and does not allow Black to play Qb4+, intending the trade of queens. There is only one sound choice: 11)...Nbd7 (Diagram 3.22). Black allows the knight on b8 to be part of the game, simultaneously blocking White's check. Do you remember what to do now? If you skipped Chapter 2, shame on you. I forgive you, but can you find the move? Don't forget the elements.

Diagram 3.21: Position after 11)Bxb5+.   Diagram 3.22: Position after 11)...Nbd7.

The Least You Need to Know

♦ Develop as quickly as you can to have more soldiers join the fight.

♦ With more space, it is easier to maneuver pieces.

♦ Material means little if you will end up checkmated.

♦ Don't be afraid to give up material if you will checkmate your opponent as a result.

Part 2

1)e4 Openings

Now that you've seen notation and the five elements, we are going to look at some specific openings. In this part, we will dive into openings that begin with White's first move of 1)e4. Each and every variation will attempt to apply the elements in some way.

Since 1)e4 is the most played move of all time, there's been a lot of trial and error. So I will bring you up-to-date with more current moves played by the best of the best. We will also analyze some variations, which might not follow our principles so well.

Chapter 4

1)e4 e5

In This Chapter

- ◆ Petrov Defense
- ◆ Scotch Game
- ◆ Italian Game

Throughout the history of chess, hundreds of openings and variations have been developed and tested. None has stood the test of time like e4. The move 1)e4 has been the true benchmark for all openings. This move has been championed and promoted by the majority of World Champions. It was even the primary weapon for Bobby Fischer—arguably the greatest chess player in the game's existence. These are wonderful footsteps to follow in.

What makes 1)e4 the most highly regarded of all time? In Chapter 3, we discussed the effectiveness of e4. Use the elements! It stamps its presence in the center and frees squares for the bishop and queen (space and time). If you look ahead, it is possible to castle by the fourth move if 1)e4 is played (king safety). No first move can allow you to castle quicker than 1)e4—only tie. A very element-satisfying move indeed! The Black side must find a suitable reaction. Black can mimic White's idea and play 1)...e5. Notice that this move applies the elements in an identical fashion as 1)e4. It also discourages White from playing 2)d4, building a classic center (which can be gained by controlling the four central squares with two pawns).

For centuries, 1)e4 e5 was the "only way" to start off a chess game. Back in the day, this was standard because it was based on logical principles similar to the elements, determined by the world's best players. After 1)...e5 many ideas were tried, but only some were successful. That's why I prefer to focus on the moves that are in sync with the five elements and that offer the simplest route to a playable position. I will also take a look at some popular variations you need to know. All the games in Chapter 4 will begin 1)e4 e5 (Diagram 4.1). After we explore this starting position and the different branches, you should be confident enough to play these positions from either side.

Diagram 4.1: Position after 1)e4 e5.

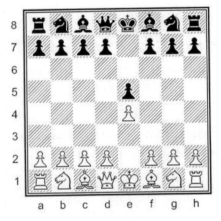

Petrov Defense

The Petrov or Petroff Defense is characterized by an overall solid position, conceding a small amount of space to White. These attributes give this opening the reputation of a reliable defense. When top Grandmasters need a draw, the Petrov is an opening they often opt to play. The game begins 1)e4 e5 2)Nf3 attacking the e5 pawn. Black plays 2)...Nf6, launching the Petrov Defense (Diagram 4.2).

Black is unfazed by White's threat and believes in "an eye for an eye" by threatening White's pawn on e5. From here, White can take a few different roads. White's main move is 3)Nxe5, seen in Diagram 4.3. The pawn is taken without hesitation. Black's original thought was to play 3)...Nxe4, but is there a flaw in this copycat move?

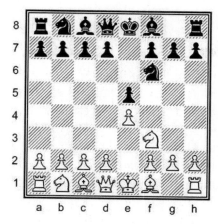

Diagram 4.2: Position after 2)...Nf6.

Diagram 4.3: Position after 3)Nxe5.

 Watch Out! _____

Black's optimistic 3)...Nxe4?! leads to unsatisfactory positions. White can play the trap-setting 4)Qe2, attacking Black's knight. Black moves 4)...Nf6 to bring the knight to safety, and White responds with the devastating discovered attack 5)Nc6+, putting the Black king in check and threatening the queen. No matter how Black responds here, the queen is lost. Instead of the blind 4)...Nf6, Black's best is 4)...Qe7. A logical game continuation is 5)Qxe4 d6 6)d4 dxe5 7)dxe5 Nc6 8)Bb5 Bd7 9)Nc3 0-0-0 10)Bf4, leaving White up a pawn and in better position. Black is worse off here, but this beats parting with the queen.

Black should play the superior 3)...d6. Then White plays 4)Nf3, retreating the knight, and Black can safely move 4)...Nxe4, taking the pawn (Diagram 4.4). However, Black should be very attentive over the next few moves.

Black takes the pawn with bravery. If White plays 5)Qe2 now, Black defends just fine with 5)...Qe7. The main line of this system is to play the central advance 5)d4. A frequented line is 5)...d5 6)Bd3 Nc6 7)0-0 Be7 8)c4 Nb4 9)Be2 0-0 10)Nc3 Bf5 11)a3 Nxc3 12)bxc3 Nc6 13)Re1 Re8 14)cxd5 cxd5 15)Bf4 Rac8. That's quite a lot, and it does not end there. Sure, you could play this, but I recommend a much simpler approach. You should try 5)Nc3 (Diagram 4.5). World-class players, including the current World Champion Viswanathan Anand, have had success with 5)Nc3.

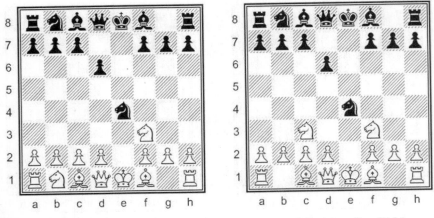

Diagram 4.4: Position after 4)...Nxe4.   Diagram 4.5: Position after 5)Nc3.

White challenges Black's knight in the center. If Black backs the knight up, time and space will be lost. So Black simply trades knights to avoid disobeying the elements with 5)...Nxc3. Why should Black avoid playing the natural looking 5)...Bf5 instead? Then White plays 6)dxc3, freeing the bishop on c1. White has doubled c-pawns, but the pieces are more active as a result. Next, Black hustles to castle by playing 6)...Be7. White follows up by playing 7)Bf4, possibly preventing the Black knight from going to e5. Black continues with 7)...0-0, and White plays 8)Qd2 (Diagram 4.6).

Diagram 4.6: Position after 8)Qd2.

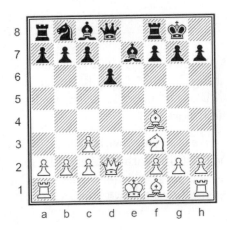

Watch Out!

After 5)Nc3, Black should not play 5)...Bf5. White will pin this knight 6)Qe2, threatening to win a piece. Black can play 6)...d5, but that runs into 7)d3 winning the knight on e4. Other than 6)...d5, Black can protect the knight with 6)...Qe7, but after 7)Nd5! Black is lost. If Black plays 7)...Qe6, this holds on to the knight but loses the queen to 8)Nxc7+. Also, if Black tries 7)...Qd7, this fails to 8)d3. Ironically, it was Anand who fell into this trap in the late 1980s.

White plans on castling queenside and wishes to build up an attack on Black's kingside. Black can continue 8)...Nd7, heading to c5 (space). The bishop on c8 is blocked for only a short time. The game can move forward with 9)0-0-0 Nc5. Both sides have arranged most of their army, except their light-squared bishops.

Scotch Game

In the Scotch Game, White plans to exchange blows in the center to gain space, but it takes time for White to solidify the middle of the board. The Scotch is entered after 1)e4 e5 2)Nf3 Nc6 3)d4 (Diagram 4.7).

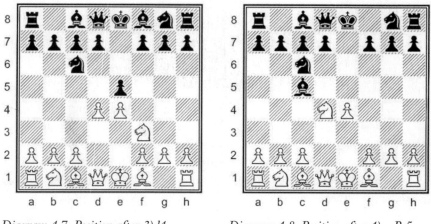

Diagram 4.7: Position after 3)d4.   *Diagram 4.8: Position after 4)...Bc5.*

3)d4 attempts to win Black's pawn on e5 and opens up the bishop. Black plays 3)...exd4 to get rid of this threat. Then White moves 4)Nxd4, centralizing the knight and regaining the pawn. To do this, White had to make two knight moves, allowing Black to gain time. Black plays the most fundamental move: 4)...Bc5 (Diagram 4.8). The bishop is given life, and it threatens to end the life of White's knight. Black should refrain from playing 4)...Nxd4?!, moving the knight twice. White will move 5)Qxd4, placing the queen in the center and interfering with Black's mobilization.

Black can also play 4)...Nf6 or even 4)...Qh4, but these can become quite complicated and lengthy. I like the very solid 4)...Bc5 because it forces White to respond to the threat on the knight at d4. White reacts most effectively by playing 5)Be3, developing and defending (Diagram 4.9). Another possible move for White is to play 5)Nxc6. Black could play 5)...bxc6, but better is the *intermezzo* 5)...Qf6. The queen move threatens checkmate on the spot, and Black can capture the knight after White defends mate. For example, 6)Qf3 dxc6 and the game is roughly equal.

Diagram 4.9: Position after 5)Be3.

<table>
<tr><td></td></tr>
</table>

Chess Language

An **intermezzo** is an in-between move. Instead of making the automatic capture, a different move is played first. Another name is *zwischenzug*, the German word for an in-between move.

Returning to 5)Be3 (Diagram 4.9), Black can keep White on his toes with 5)...Qf6, hoping to win the knight on d4. White plays 6)c3 to safeguard the knight, and Black plays 6)...Nge7, introducing the knight into the game. A natural continuation is 7)Bc4 Ne5 8)Be2 d5 9)Nd2 0-0 10)0-0 Bb6, where White and Black can be content with their current positions.

Italian Game

Pedro Damiano was the first to play the Italian Game, but this opening borrows the name of the Italian chess player and author Gioachino
Greco, who studied this game and published analysis on these positions.

The Italian Game begins 1)e4 e5 2)Nf3 Nc6 3)Bc4 (Diagram 4.10).
These moves have been recorded in games dating back to the early
1500s. The Italian Game may be ancient, but it's still full of venom if
one is not prepared. What are the motives behind 3)Bc4? White targets
the f7 square and possibly the g8 square if Black castles kingside. The
bishop cuts across the center, thus preventing d5 by Black. Also, White
is ready to castle. Overall, 3)Bc4 uses the elements, and it has aggressive
intentions to go after Black's king. Black has two principled and popular
responses: 3)…Bc5 or 3)…Nf6.

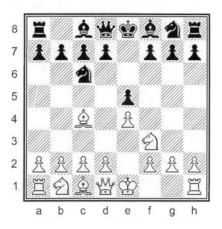

*Diagram 4.10: Position
after 3)Bc4.*

3)…Bc5

In Diagram 4.11, Black plays 3)…Bc5, having similar ideas to White's
last move. We have reached a position played countless times, and
White has three main options. One way for White to proceed is 4)c3—
the Giuoco Piano. The others are 4)b4 (Evans Gambit) and 4)0-0.

In Diagram 4.12, White plays 4)c3 supporting a future d4 push. There
is also a reserve idea of playing b4, gaining space on the queenside.
Black plays the natural 4)…Nf6, attacking e4 with a tempo and making castling available. White sticks to the initial plan and plays 5)d4
(Diagram 4.13).

Diagram 4.11: Position after 3)...Bc5.

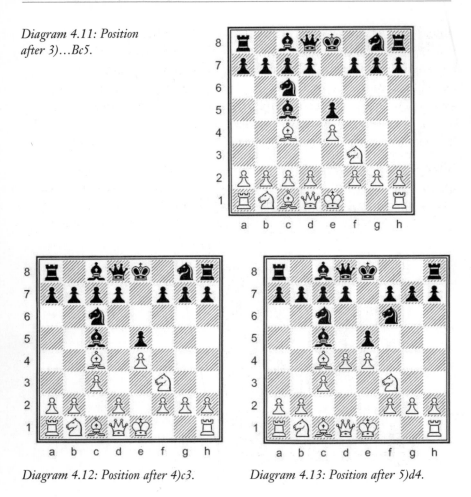

Diagram 4.12: Position after 4)c3.   *Diagram 4.13: Position after 5)d4.*

This pawn move attempts to seize space by forcing back Black's pieces. It also gives the bishop on c1 squares to roam. This is White's most direct plan, but for specific reasons it does not appear to be the best. 5)d4 is premature due to 5)...exd4 6)cxd4 Bb4+ 7)Bd2 Bxd2+. {Also, 7)...Nxe4 8)Bxb4 Nxb4 9)Bxf7+ Kxf7 10)Qb3+ d5 11) Ne5+?! Ke6 12)Qxb4 c5 and Black is most likely better here.} 8)Nbxd2 d5 challenging the center 9)exd5 Nxd5 10)Qb3 Na5 11)Qa4+ Nc6 and White can repeat moves to gain a draw. Even if White plays other moves on move 10 or 11, Black's position is at least equal to White's. Is that what White really wants?

Let's try to figure out the best plan. First of all, Black is attacking the pawn on e4 after 4)...Nf6, so White could play 5)d3 protecting the pawn instead of 5)d4. White would like to castle and use d4 at the right time. The purpose of delaying d4 is to avoid Bb4 being a check as in the 5)d4 line. A sample line after 5)d3 is 5)...d6 cementing the e5 pawn and then 6)0-0 0-0 7)a4. The move 7)a4 is a seemingly useless move, but White can win a piece if Black plays a normal developing move such as 7)...Bg4?. The rest would play out 8)b4 Bb6 9)a5 and White wins a piece. A smarter move for Black is 7)...a5 stopping b4, and Black has obtained a suitable game.

After 3)...Bc5, White can also try 4)b4!? entering the entertaining Evans Gambit (Diagram 4.14). This pawn gambit is an attempt to gain control of the center by diverting Black's bishop away from the middle of the board. In addition, White will have a modest space advantage and lead in time, but is this enough after 4)...Bxb4?

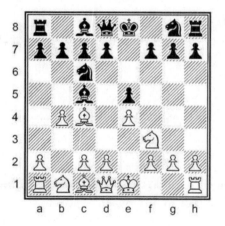

Diagram 4.14: Position after 4)b4!?

![King icon] **The Chess Sage**

To be objective, I hardly doubt that the Evans Gambit is better for White if Black plays accurately. The top Grandmasters in the world rarely ever play this as White. Many times, this is an indication that a particular opening is not sound, or it does not offer good winning chances against an informed opponent. However, if Black is not prepared, one can end up in a lost position very quickly.

Now White must show that parting with the pawn was worth it. By far, the most logical and common move by White is 5)c3. This puts a question to Black's bishop on b4 and will serve as a stepping stone for playing d4. There are four decent variations to choose from, but I

Chess Language

A strategy used in response to a disadvantage or weakness can be defined as **counterplay**.

believe that 5)...Bd6 is simplest to play and offers Black a chance to dodge countless theory and computer analysis (Diagram 4.15). The main line is really 5)...Ba5, but this can be very complex, and I believe it gives White sufficient *counterplay* for the lost pawn.

Diagram 4.15: Position after 5)...Bd6.

This bishop move is known as the Stone-Ware Defense. The bishop on d6 is not very active, but it helps nail down the e5 square. White will most likely play 6)d4, when Black should play 6)...Nf6 to develop the knight and attack the e4 pawn. Some games have continued 7)0-0 0-0 8)Re1 h6, stopping the bishop or knight from going to g5, and then 9)Nbd2 Re8 10)Qb3 Qe7 and Black's position is solid (Diagram 4.16). White is down a pawn, but Black's position is somewhat cramped, and the bishop on c8 has no available squares. I would assess this as an unclear position with chances for both sides.

Refer to Diagram 4.11. There is still one more variation to look at after 3)...Bc5. White can respond to this move with 4)0-0 (Diagram 4.17). Here, Black's best bet is to stick to the fundamental 4)...Nf6. The safe move 5)d3 can be played by White, but this line is not as dangerous for Black. A route to force Black to play accurately and aggressively is 5)d4. White gambits a pawn to hold back Black's development. The most dependable counter is 5)...exd4. White is on the prowl for more space and plays 6)e5, planning to dislodge Black's knight to a poor square.

Now the Max Lange Attack begins. Black does not have to attend to the knight on f6. Instead, Black plays 6)...d5, attacking White's bishop on c4 (Diagram 4.18).

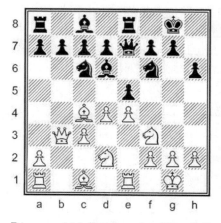

Diagram 4.16: Position after 10)...Qe7.   *Diagram 4.17: Position after 4)0-0.*

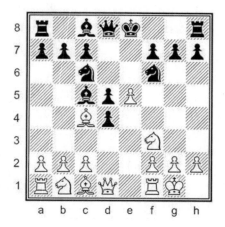

Diagram 4.18: Position after 6)...d5.

These positions become exceedingly unclear and can even be mismanaged by Grandmasters. Therefore, I would suggest you steer clear from these lines unless you feel like living on the edge. The classical main line is 7)exf6 dxc4 8)Re1 Be6+ 9)Ng5 {threatening 10)Nxe6 fxe6 11)Qh5+} Qd5 10)Nc3 Qf5 11)Nce4 0-0-0, and the position is quite messy (Diagram 4.19). I have won some nice games in this position as White, but my opponents made mistakes along the way. I have also cross-checked this line with a few of the top computer programs in the world, and no real advantage is given to White or Black, although

Chess Language

If the same position has repeated itself and it's the same player's turn to move each time, no matter what happened in-between, a draw can be claimed by **threefold repetition**.

White does have an interesting forced draw line after 12)g4 Qe5 13)Nf3 Qd5 14)fxg7 Rhg8 16)Ne4 Qd5 17)Nf6 Qd6 18)Ne4 Qd5 *threefold repetition*. A common perspective seems to be if Black plays precisely, White has no advantage. Arguments can be made for either side, but I'll take a rain check!

Diagram 4.19: Position after 11)...0-0-0.

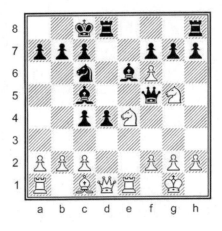

3...Nf6

The Two Knights Defense is reached after 3)...Nf6 (Diagram 4.20). Black eyeballs the pawn on e4, hoping to slow down White's development. White goes for the kill immediately with 4)Ng5 (Diagram 4.21). The knight threatens to capture the pawn on f7, forking the queen and rook. How does Black cope with this threat?

Diagram 4.20: Position after 3)...Nf6.

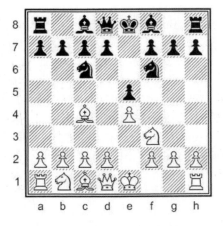

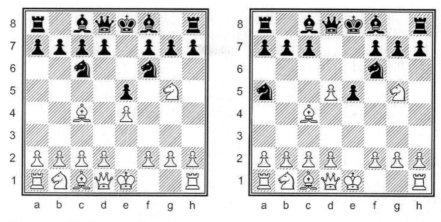

Diagram 4.21: Position after 4)Ng5.   *Diagram 4.22: Position after 5)...Na5.*

The f7 square should be defended. The most effective way to do this is to play 4)...d5 and obstruct White's bishop on c4. The combative pawn move also opens up squares for the bishop on c8. White destroys Black's pawn with 5)exd5, and Black plays 5)...Na5 chasing White's bishop (Diagram 4.22). Black's fifth move is most popular in Grandmaster play.

The Chess Sage

As an alternative to 4)...d5, Black can try the fearless 4)...Bc5, known as the Traxler Gambit or Wilkes-Barre Variation. White can gain material with 5)Nxf7, but Black builds up an unrelenting attack. I truly believe the complexities are beyond the scope of this book, and if you chose to play this, please research this opening heavily. This means if you have the White pieces and play 4)Ng5, you have to be prepared for an opponent who just might try 4)...Bc5.

Otherwise, Black could play the obvious 5)...Nxd5. Then White could play the testing gambit 6)Nxf7—Fried Liver Attack. The practically forced series of moves are 6)...Kxf7 7)Qf3+ Ke6 8)Nc3 Ne7 {or 8)...Nb4} 9)d4 c6, protecting the knight on d5. On the surface, Black nets a piece for a pawn. Unfortunately, Black's king has to dodge bullets and defend near flawlessly to survive. I think it is a poor practical choice to play 5)...Nxd5?! because it might not be sound and requires so much accuracy. Also, White has another strong move in the arsenal instead of 6)Nxf7. It is not necessary to gambit a piece, so White could opt for 6)d4, which may be objectively stronger than 6)Nxf7.

Take a look back at Diagram 4.22. What should White do here? White plays 6)Bb5+, moving the bishop to a safe square and simultaneously putting the Black king in check. One line continues 6)...c6 7)dxc6 bxc6 8)Be2 h6 9)Nh3 Bc5 (Diagram 4.23).

Diagram 4.23: Position after 9)...Bc5.

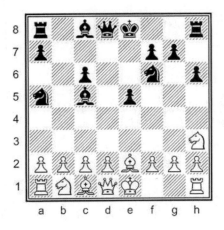

In the grand scheme of things, Black is down a pawn but dominates the space on the board. In Diagram 4.23, White has not moved a single piece on the queenside, and Black is almost done developing (time). White is up a pawn, and Black has an isolated a-pawn and c-pawn (pawn structure). A fair assessment would be that this position is dynamically equal. Definitely nobody is losing here, and the better chess player should be victorious with either side of this position.

The Least You Need to Know

◆ Use the elements in conjunction with concrete analysis.

◆ You must be prepared, especially for openings with gambits.

◆ Don't play for tricks, be objective.

◆ If these openings don't suit your tastes, there are other options!

Chapter 5

Ruy Lopez

In This Chapter

- ◆ Alternatives to the main lines
- ◆ The early exchange
- ◆ The best-known moves

In the jungle of openings, the Ruy Lopez is the king. Since approximately the sixteenth century, no opening has remained as popular as the Ruy Lopez. The name originates from the Spanish priest Ruy Lopez de Segura, who did a study of the opening.

Amongst all the openings, the Ruy Lopez has the reputation of being the elite choice to gain an advantage. The top players in the world continuously clash in the king of open games, searching for the truth of the position. The consensus is that White obtains an edge in the opening, but the complete road to winning the game is yet to be discovered. I will discuss the most principled options and reveal the concepts behind the most commonly played variations. I will by no means try to "solve" this opening; rather, I will give you the essentials necessary to reach a playable position. Then you will be ready to play the Ruy Lopez.

The Ruy Lopez begins 1)e4, gaining space in the center and opening pathways for the bishop and queen. Black shadows White with 1)...e5, which has the same benefits as White's first move. Then White targets a central pawn while developing a piece by 2)Nf3. Black plays 2)...Nc6, defending the pawn on e5. Here, White continues the pressure with 3)Bb5 (Diagram 5.1). This move does not break any of the elements. This places pressure on the knight on c6, indirectly contending for the center. White now has the freedom to castle and swiftly complete the mobilization of his or her forces. Diagram 5.1 is the starting position of the Ruy Lopez. Overall, the Ruy Lopez is one big battle royale for the domination of the center.

Diagram 5.1: Position after 3)Bb5.

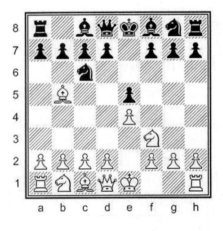

Side of the Ruy

Following 3)Bb5, Black has quite a few options to the main line, but I will narrow these to what I believe best suits the five elements.

3)...Bc5

Black plays 3)...Bc5 to move a piece out into the fight, preventing the central thrust—4)d4 and helping Black to castle (Diagram 5.2). White can't win a pawn by removing the sole defender of the e5 pawn. If 4)Bxc6 dxc6 5)Nxe5, Black will counterattack with 5)...Qd4, centralizing the queen. This creates three threats in White's position: the pawn on e4, the knight on e5, and most importantly, checkmate on f2.

White's most resourceful move is 6)Nd3, saving the knight and using this knight to defend the f2 square. Black will then play 6)...Qxe4+, regaining the pawn and securing a nice position.

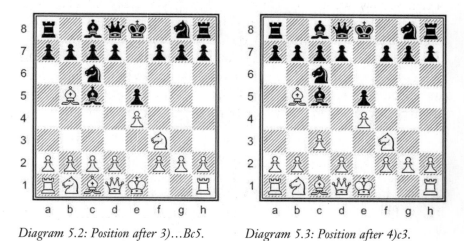

Diagram 5.2: Position after 3)...Bc5.   Diagram 5.3: Position after 4)c3.

In Diagram 5.3, White plays 4)c3 to help control the d4 square, preparing to expand in the center with 5)d4 {5)0-0 is a solid and popular choice}. Black proceeds with 4)...Nf6 attacking the e4 pawn and clearing up the remaining square to castle. 5)d4 is played as planned. This puts a question to the bishop on c5 and attacks e5, overtakes the center, and grants a diagonal for the bishop on c1 to roam. Black temporarily removes the threat of the bishop on c5 and captures with the pawn being attacked 5)...exd4. However, 5)...Bb6 may be objectively better.

White does not have to capture the pawn on d4 first. In Diagram 5.4, White plays an intermezzo by 6)e5. The aim of this move is to displace the Black knight to an unfavorable square. This still allows White to capture the pawn on d4 after Black's knight is moved. Black plays 6)... Ne4, actively controlling squares in White's camp. This piece enters no man's land, but can the knight be forced into submission? White could try 7)Qe2 to exploit the lone knight. 7)...d5 is the only good way to defend the knight. Then the logical move for White is 8)exd6 e.p., getting rid of the knight's only defender. Black plays 8)...Bf5, and White adds another attacker to the pinned knight on e4 with 9)Nbd2?. Does Black lose the knight? No, Black ignores this by playing 9)...0-0. After 10)Nxe4 Bxe4, White can't play 11)Qxe4 because of 11)...Re8 pinning and winning the queen. Only Black profits from the complications.

Diagram 5.4: Position after 6)e5.

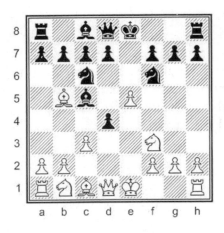

After 6)...Ne4, White plays the patient and powerful 7)0-0 (Diagram 5.5). The hidden point of this move is to play 8)cxd4 without allowing 8)...Bb4 to be a check. If White had thoughtlessly played 7)cxd4, Black could continue with 7)...Bb4+, having no opening difficulties. In Diagram 5.6, Black reacts with 7)...d5, providing support for the knight on e4 and giving the bishop on c8 air. The greedy 7)...dxc3?! can allow White to gain time and space. For example, 8)Qd5 c2 9)Qxe4 cxb1Q 10)Rxb1 0-0?! 11)Bd3 threatens checkmate 11)...g6 12)Bh6 Re8 13)Bc4. All of White's pieces are in the game, and Black has an inactive bishop on c8 and rook on a8. Due to these factors, White's position is preferable despite being down a pawn.

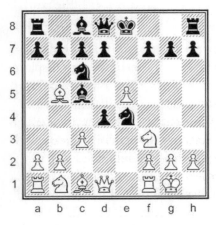

Diagram 5.5: Position after 7)0-0.

Diagram 5.6: Position after 7)...d5.

In Diagram 5.7, White plays 8)cxd4. Black can play 8)...Bb6 to move the bishop to safety while still keeping an eye on d4. If we try to assess the position after 8)...Bb6, it is a fairly level game. White has two pieces developed and has castled. In comparison, Black has three pieces out in the game and can castle very shortly. If anything, White has a slight plus because of more space in the center, but Black still has a playable position.

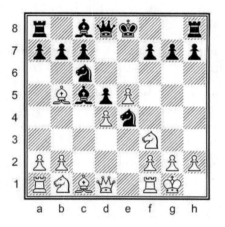

Diagram 5.7: Position after 8)cxd4.

Let's refer to Diagram 5.6, the position after 7)...d5. Instead of White playing the solid 8)cxd4, White could try the enterprising 8)exd6 e.p. Thereafter, Black should play 8)...0-0, then 9)dxc7 Qxc7 10)cxd4 Rd8 11)Qc2!, and it appears White is on top. If you are not comfortable playing these lines with Black, the main lines may be a better choice for you.

Berlin: 3)...Nf6

First played in Berlin, the Berlin Defense is known for its resiliency and impenetrable nature against White's army. This defense commences when Black confronts White's approach by putting the e4 pawn under fire and plays 3)...Nf6 (Diagram 5.8). Black hopes that White will directly defend the pawn, slowing down White's development. Moves like 4)Nc3 or 4)d3 relinquish partial control over the d4 square. Black can play 4)...Bc5 after either of these moves and should find it easier to reach a suitable middlegame.

In Diagram 5.9, White responds with 4)0-0 and ignores Black's possibility of 4)...Nxe4. The move 4)0-0 secures the king's position while transferring the rook in the game. Black plays 4)...Nxe4 and says "Prove it." The game continues 5)d4, but what about the logical 5)Re1? This move attacks the knight on e4 and threatens to win the e5 pawn later. It meets the criteria of the five elements: White develops the rook with a tempo and gains space in the center. I believe 5)Re1 offers White the chance for a small advantage. Play continues 5)...Nd6 6)Nxe5 Be7 {6)...Nxb5?? 7)Nxc6+ and Black's queen is lost} 7)Bf1 Nxe5 8)Rxe5 0-0 9)d4 Bf6 10)Re1 Nf5 11)c3 d5 12)Bd3, and White finds it easier to situate his or her pieces.

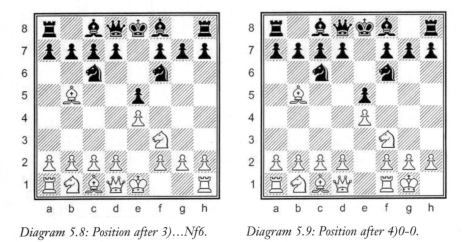

Diagram 5.8: Position after 3)...Nf6.   Diagram 5.9: Position after 4)0-0.

Black needs to pay for the insolence, and White plays the central strike 5)d4 (Diagram 5.10). White intends to pry open the center while Black's king is susceptible to a siege on the e-file. Moves like 6)dxe5 and 6)Re1 are in White's arsenal. Black anticipates 6)Re1 and counters with 5)...Nd6, attacking the bishop on b5. The play continues 6)Bxc6 dxc6 7)dxe5, threatening the knight on d6—the best capture. When the knight moves this will allow queen trades, taking away Black's chance to castle.

Black finds the safest square for the knight by playing 7)...Nf5 (Diagram 5.11). Other tries for Black such as 7)...Ne4 or 7)...Nc4 result in the knight being chased by 8)Qe2. 8)Qxd8 can also be played, leading to a similar position as the game. The only other legal knight move 7)...Nb5 loses the knight to 8)a4. Oops!

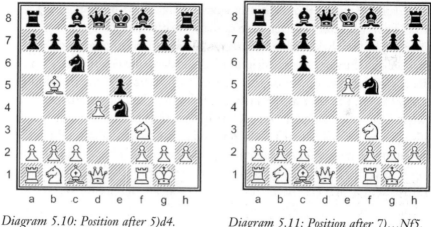

Diagram 5.10: Position after 5)d4.   *Diagram 5.11: Position after 7)...Nf5.*

In Diagram 5.12, the main goal of 8)Qxd8+ is to force the king to move so that castling is no longer legal. Black must play 8)...Kxd8 (Diagram 5.13). We have reached a very well-known position in Diagram 5.13. Edward Lasker, the second World Champion, played and considered this a solid defense for Black. In recent times, the Classical World Champion (2000–2006) and Undisputed World Champion (2006–2007) Vladimir Kramnik used this as his main defense to baffle former World Champion (1985–1993) and Classical World Champion (1993–2000) Garry Kasparov. Kramnik did not lose a game in the entire match, and much of this was due to his impenetrable Berlin Defense. So what is the big deal with this opening?

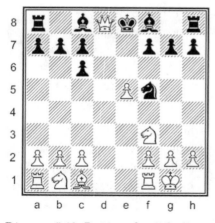

Diagram 5.12: Position after 8)Qxd8+.

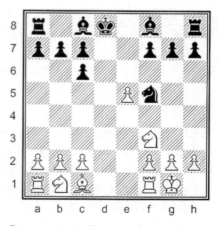

Diagram 5.13: Position after 8)...Kxd8.

If we fully examine the position in Diagram 5.13, White may have a small advantage, but is it enough to win? White has a bit of a lead in time, and Black has doubled c-pawns. Black can no longer castle, but without queens on the board it is much harder to expose Black's king. Black's compensation lies within the bishop pair. Since the position is mostly open, the bishops will have more power and range (space). Also, two bishops can complement each other on the colored squares that the other bishop can't. Since White no longer has a light-squared bishop, the light squares will become considerably weaker. This is why, at the top levels, this has been a position extremely difficult for White to win. This is why I suggest the principled 5)Re1 as an alternative to avoid this theoretical debate, which offers just as many practical winning chances.

Exchange Variation: 4)Bxc6

The Ruy Lopez begins 1)e4 e5 2)Nf3 Nc6 3)Bb5. The most popular choice remains 3)...a6 (Diagram 5.14). Does this follow the principles? The a6 pawn forces the White bishop to make a concession. If White moves 4)Ba4, Black basically includes 3)...a6 for free. If White plays 4)Bxc6, then we will reach the Exchange Variation (Diagram 5.15). White concedes the light-squared bishop but creates double c-pawns for Black. Black recaptures by 4)...dxc6. This is the most logical capture. This gives the bishop scope on the c8 to h3 diagonal and opens up additional squares for the queen to control on the d-file. Now White plays 5)0-0 (Diagram 5.16).

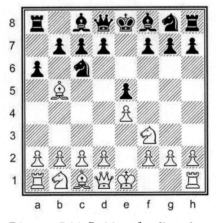

Diagram 5.14: Position after 3)...a6.

Diagram 5.15: Position after 4)Bxc6.

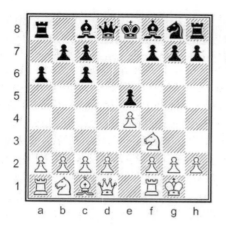

Diagram 5.16: Position after 5)0-0.

White tucks the king away before fighting for the center. Why was 5)Nxe5 not a wise choice? Black would play 5)...Qd4, creating dual threats on the pawn on e4 and the knight on e5 (double attack). White would most likely move the knight, and Black would take the pawn on e4. Black would easily mobilize his or her forces and should be free of any opening headaches. Continuing with the game, after 5)0-0 Black plays 5)...Bg4. This pins the knight, making use of the bishop on the first available chance. White would like to remove this nuisance and plays 6)h3 to be rid of the pest. Should Black capture the knight on f3 or retreat the bishop?

Neither! Black responds with the shocking 6)...h5!? (Diagram 5.17). At first, the pawn move seems to be a waste of time, disobeying one of the five elements. This is a move that relies purely on tactical resources and the position of the White king (king safety). A quick glance would suggest Black has given away the bishop for no good reason. In reality, the bishop on g4 is currently immune from being captured. If White makes the reasonable-looking capture 7)hxg4, this will open up the h-file for the Black rook on h8 after 7)...hxg4. White can move the attacked knight and hunt for more material with 8)Nxe5??. {8)d3 is best, but after 8)...gxf3 9)Qxf3 Qh4 10)Qh3 Qxh3 11)gxh3 Rxh3, Black has a desirable position being a pawn up.} Now Black has an avenue (the h-file) to the exposed White king. Black can play the menacing 8)...Qh4, threatening checkmate by 9)...Qh2 or 9)...Qh1 checkmate. White must create an escape route for the king, so 9)f3 is played. White now plans on placing the king on f2 after either queen check. Logically, Black cuts off the escape square with 9)...g3. The White king has no access to the f2 square, and checkmate is inevitable. White could try 10)Ng4, and Black would follow with 10)...Qh1 checkmate. The move 10)...Qh2+ does not work because the knight on g4 controls the h2 square.

White avoids these consequences and plays a quiet, useful move: 7)d3 (Diagram 5.18). Squares are opened to the bishop on c1, and the knight on b1 is given an additional square to utilize. Black follows up with the unconventional 7)...Qf6, creating the option to castle on the queenside. The true aim of this move is to play 8)...Bxf3 9)Qxf3 Qxf3 10)gxf3, deconstructing White's pawn structure: doubled f-pawns and an isolated h-pawn are created. To avoid these pawn weaknesses, White plays 8)Nbd2. So, if Black plays 8)...Bxf3, White could retake the bishop by 9)Nxf3, maintaining the pawn structure.

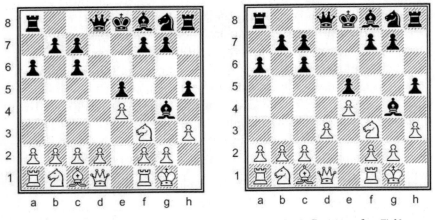

Diagram 5.17: Position after 6)...h5.   *Diagram 5.18: Position after 7)d3.*

Alternatively, if White played 8)Be3, the game would continue 8)...Bxf3 9)Qxf3 Qxf3 10)gxf3 Bd6. Both sides would have mutual doubled pawns, but White would have an isolated h-pawn. At a minimum, Black has an equal position.

In Diagram 5.19, after 7)...Qf6 8)Nbd2 Black plays 8)...Ne7 to ultimately reach the f4 square via g6. The game could continue 9)Re1 Ng6, and the knight is headed to f4. Then 10)d4 Nf4! 11)dxe5 Qg6 12)Nh4 Bxd1 13)Nxg6 Nxg6 14)Rxd1 0-0-0 results in a balanced position.

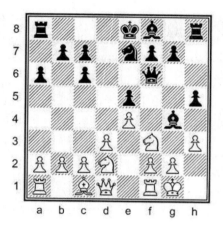

Diagram 5.19: Position after 8)...Ne7.

I suspect that you have a few questions about these moves. Can Black continue to leave the bishop on g4 *en prise?* Up until move 12, White has the opportunity to eliminate the bishop from the game. Concrete analysis reveals that White would end up fighting for equality at best if the bishop on g4 is captured between moves 7 and 12. If you would like to know the complexities, visit www. willthethrillaramil.com.

Chess Language

The phrase **en prise** is French for leaving a piece unprotected and susceptible to being captured.

The Main Game

By capturing the knight on c6 (Exchange Variation), White loses strength on the light squares and allows Black to develop more freely. The trend for the best players in the world is to keep this bishop on the board. Therefore, the suggested move is 4)Ba4, maintaining the tension in the position. White plays 4)Ba4, entering the main line of the Ruy Lopez (Diagram 5.20). It retreats the bishop but helps watch the knight influencing the center. Then Black responds with 4)...Nf6 in tune with the elements (Diagram 5.21). The knight on f6 is positioned to attack the central squares, including the e4 pawn.

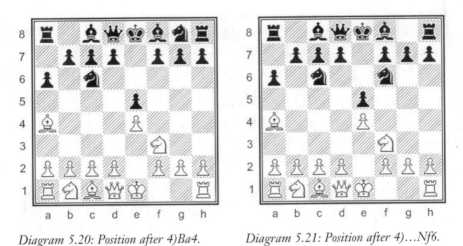

Diagram 5.20: Position after 4)Ba4.   *Diagram 5.21: Position after 4)...Nf6.*

In Diagram 5.22, White plays 5)0-0, helping king safety, and activates the rook. Black can proceed with 5)...Nxe4 (Open Variation) and White's main response is 6)d4 blasting open the center. This variation remains playable for Black, but Black has a more reserved approach in mind. Black plays the modest 5)...Be7 (Diagram 5.23). It may not be the most aggressive move, but it meets the demands of the position. Black prepares to castle and then will continue central operations. What about the logical 5)...Bc5 helping to lock down the d4 square? White can play 6)Nxe5! and then 6)...Nxe5 7)d4!, forking the knight and bishop (watch out for this fork trick!). After 7)...Bxd4 8)Qxd4, White has emerged with an excellent position.

Diagram 5.22: Position after 5)0-0.   *Diagram 5.23: Position after 5)...Be7.*

After 5)...Be7, White makes use of the rook immediately with 6)Re1 (Diagram 5.24). This does not merely protect the e4 pawn. If Black were to play the automatic move 6)...0-0, White could cash in with 7)Bxc6 dxc6 8)Nxe5, winning the center pawn. Then 8)...Qd4 fails to 9)Nf3 attacking the queen. Black foresees these problems and plays 6)...b5, forcing the bishop back while gaining space on the queenside (Diagram 5.25). In Diagram 5.26, White responds with 7)Bb3—the only move. The bishop is redeployed to a useful diagonal that cuts through the center and aims at the f7 square.

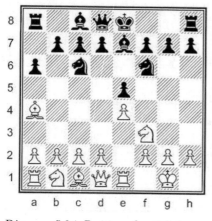

Diagram 5.24: Position after 6)Re1.

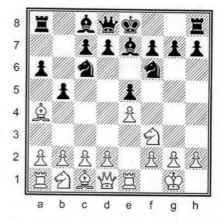

Diagram 5.25: Position after 6)...b5.

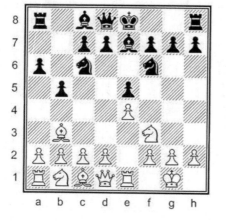

Diagram 5.26: Position after 7)Bb3.

Black wisely shields his king behind his pawns with 7)...0-0 (Diagram 5.27). Most of Black's army has been mobilized and is ready to march into the middle of the battlefield. In Diagram 5.28, White plays the most popular move 8)c3. The idea of this is to assist the pawn lunge d4. 8)c3 is the most favored attempt to dominate the center.

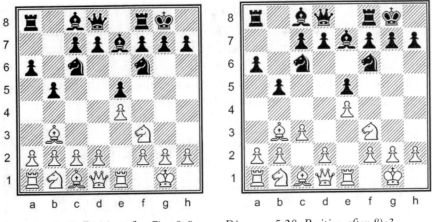

Diagram 5.27: Position after 7)...0-0.   *Diagram 5.28: Position after 8)c3.*

We are at a crossroads of two popular choices. In Diagram 5.29, Black plays 8)...d6, considered to be the most solid choice. This move is designed to reinforce the e5 pawn and add a path for the bishop on c8 to reach g4. Since the White knight plays a significant role in the central conflict, Black hopes to pin and neutralize the knight with 9)...Bg4.

Diagram 5.29: Position after 8)...d6.

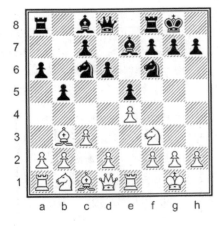

The Chess Sage

Instead of 8)...d6, Black can try the legendary Marshall Attack. There is more than enough material to write a book about this gambit, but I will show you the initial strikes. The Marshall initiates with 8)...d5. This will surrender a pawn, but Black will have other compensation. Play moves on with 9)exd5 Nxd5 10)Nxe5 Nxe5 11)Rxe5 c6. Black is down one pawn but has a very spacious position. Also, it will take White at least two moves to develop the bishop on c1, and the knight can only move to the side of the board on a3. While White is trying to finish activating pieces, Black will direct an assault on White's king.

This is a highly complex position that some Grandmasters prefer to avoid. The resulting position is not necessarily worse for either side, but it is not so fun for your king to be under siege. You must be prepared for this opening, as there are many pitfalls along the way. Play at your own risk! Nonetheless, the Marshall Attack can be sidestepped. If you play 8)a4, which has been dubbed the Anti-Marshall, you will not have to worry about the dreaded Marshall Attack. On the other hand, 8)a4 does not give you the perks of the main line. Other noteworthy Anti-Marshall lines are 8)h3 and 8)a3.

After 8)...d6, White plays 9)h3 (Diagram 5.30). Does this move adhere to any of the elements? A quick glance might tell you that this is a useless move. However, it prevents the Black bishop from going to g4, pinning the knight. The knight heavily strengthens White's center, so White prevents Black from immobilizing this piece. Basically, it is a *prophylactic move* geared toward indirectly helping the center (space). Remember, the center is the key in the Ruy Lopez.

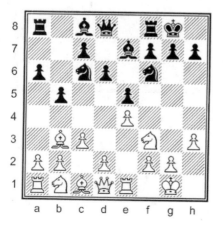

Diagram 5.30: Position after 9)h3.

A **prophylactic move** is simply a preventative measure. **Tabiya** is known today as a position that is reached so often that the real game begins after this initial series of moves. In the Ruy Lopez, the game really starts after 9)h3.

There is enough information on the Ruy Lopez that at least an entire 500-page book could be written on this opening. A large proportion of this book could be devoted to the main line. From here on out, I would like to give you the most frequently played moves. The position up to 9)h3 is a *tabiya*. After 9)h3 there are many solid options such as 9)...Bb7, 9)...Nb8, 9)...Nd7, and 9)...h6, but 9)...Na5 is most common. The knight intends to capture the light-squared bishop, and it gives way to the c-pawn. White wants to preserve this bishop and plays 10)Bc2. Then Black plays 10)...c5, taking more of a stake in center. White counters with 11)d4, threatening to win a pawn on e5, so Black protects this by playing 11)...Qc7.

All in all, both sides have reached a playable position. Many Grandmasters have victories from each side of the Ruy Lopez, revealing the "playability" of this opening. Hopefully, you have a good understanding of the reasons behind the moves of the Ruy Lopez. Now you can play it, too!

The Least You Need to Know

◆ You can't go wrong with Ruy Lopez.

◆ The initial road has been paved, but there is still much to learn.

◆ You cannot just memorize the moves, you have to apply the elements and understand the ideas of the moves.

◆ Study the games of the World Champions of the past and present.

Chapter 6

The Dynamic Sicilian

In This Chapter

◆ The Smith-Morra Gambit

◆ The Solid c3

◆ The Four Knights of the Sicilian and the Kan Variation

◆ The Sveshnikov

The Sicilian Defense, known for its unrelenting attacks, has taken over modern chess by a landslide. Since this was the favorite opening for both Bobby Fischer and Garry Kasparov (former World Champions), chess players have recognized the true power of the Sicilian. It can even be called the "home run" or "knockout" of chess because one false move and it's game over. How did the razor-sharp Sicilian Defense gain its name? It spawned from an old Italian chess work, which used the phrase "Sicilian Game." Since then, it has taken on the precise name of "Sicilian Defense."

Players are often plagued by choices in the opening that lead to boring positions, but the Sicilian Defense offers exciting play supported by the greats of the game. Before we dive into the nitty-gritty, we will look at some of the sidelines and less played variations of the Sicilian. You will have an inside view of why these moves are not the most popular. Then you can feel ready to play against the various systems and alternatives.

After 1)e4, this uncompromising defense begins with 1)...c5 (Diagram 6.1). What purpose does Black's first move serve? First, it breaks the symmetry in the position unlike 1)...e5. Also, it overlooks d4 and gains space on the queenside. This pawn move does not help develop a bishop, but Black must take a fair share of the center before White can overtake this area of the board. The basic idea for Black is to coordinate his or her pieces to maintain the center. Black does not necessarily occupy the center with its pieces; rather, it surrounds the center.

Diagram 6.1: Position after 1)...c5.

2nd Best

The main line is 2)Nf3, but there are many decent sidelines that White can try. At amateur levels 2)d4, 2)c3, and 2)Nc3 can be potent, especially if Black is unprepared. We will cover the first two, but I recommend that you study games starting with 2)Nc3.

Smith-Morra

Both Ken Smith and Pierre Morra devoted many games, analyses, articles, and books to the gambit. To be fair to the pioneers of this gambit, the opening, beginning with 1)e4 c5 2)d4, is commonly referred to as the Smith-Morra Gambit.

The purpose of 1)...c5 is to discourage 2)d4, but White plays it anyway in the Smith-Morra Gambit (Diagram 6.2). White would like to open up lines and have free mobility. Black simply plays 2)...cxd4, and it is not ideal for White to play 3)Qxd4 because this will allow Black to play 3)...Nc6, hitting the queen. So White plays the provocative 3)c3. White aims to open up the position and gain a decent lead in time. Nevertheless, Black plays 3)...dxc3 and causes White to shed a pawn.

This is Black's best try to make White justify the pawn deficit. Black falls behind in development a little in these lines, and if you are not comfortable with this you can try 3)...Nf6 {transposes to some 2)c3 lines} or 3)...d3, declining the pawn. Anyway, after 3)...dxc3, White responds with 4)Nxc3, as seen in Diagram 6.3.

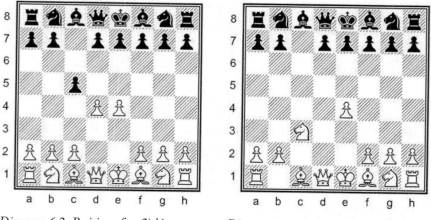

Diagram 6.2: Position after 2)d4.   *Diagram 6.3: Position after 4)Nxc3.*

Can you name the positive aspects of the position for both sides? White has diagonals for both bishops (space), the knight is well placed on c3, and White has a lead in time. Black must catch up before the king is put in danger. A continuation that may even give Black an edge is as follows: 4)...e6 5)Nf3 d6 6)Bc4 Nf6 7)Qe2 a6 8)0-0 b5 9)Bb3 Nbd7 10)Rd1 Bb7. Black is on the verge of consolidating the position with an extra pawn. However, Black must not drop his or her guard!

The c3 Sicilian

In the Smith-Morra, White deploys d4 immediately, but White can prepare this move with 2)c3—the c3 Sicilian (Diagram 6.4). The real reason behind White's move is to support the d4 pawn push. When

Black takes the d4 pawn, White will recapture with the pawn on c3. Before White can go forth using this plan, Black plays 2)...d5. {2)...Nf6 is also popular and a good line for Black to play.} In general, 2)...d5 is motivated by central play and space. The typical response for White is 3)exd5, and Black recaptures with 3)...Qxd5 having a real presence. Now White plays 4)d4 (Diagram 6.5).

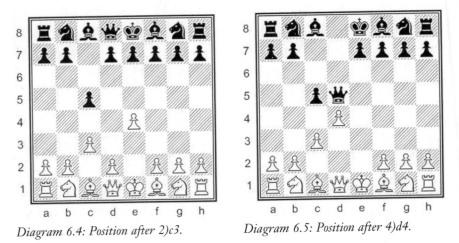

Diagram 6.4: Position after 2)c3.   Diagram 6.5: Position after 4)d4.

This move helps White gain territory, and it gives life to the bishop on c1. From here, each side follows the elements. Black plays 4)...Nc6 pressuring d4, and White defends by playing 5)Nf3. Then Black pins the knight on f3 with 5)...Bg4 and indirectly threatens to win the pawn on d4. Now White plays 6)Be2, which does not seem to help defend the d4 pawn. Black continues with 6)...cxd4, and White plays 7)cxd4. Black surprisingly plays 7)...e6 (Diagram 6.6). What if Black had continued with 7)...Bxf3 and then 8)Bxf3 Qxd4, winning a pawn?

Let's refer to Diagram 6.6. It is possible for Black to queenside castle, but it is safer on the kingside. 7)...e6 helps to develop the bishop, which will aid Black in castling kingside. The game could carry forward with 8)Nc3 attacking the queen, and Black could play 8)...Bb4, pinning the knight. White plays 9)0-0, relieving the pin and renewing the threat on Black's queen. Then Black would play 9)...Qa5, moving the queen to safety. The next game continuation is 10)h3 Bxf3 11)Bxf3 Nge7. {11)...Bxc3?! 12)bxc3 Qxc3 13)Rb1 is very dangerous for Black to play.} The game is pretty balanced after 11)...Nge7 (Diagram 6.7). White has the bishop pair but has an isolated d-pawn susceptible to attack. Black is ready to castle, and White is ready to move out the dark-squared bishop. White may have a minor space advantage, but the d-pawn could be a liability.

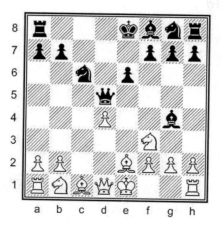

Diagram 6.6: Position after 7)...e6.

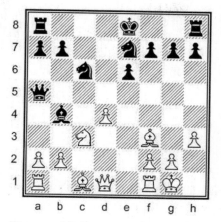

Diagram 6.7: Position after 11)...Nge7.

2)Nf3

"The Move" against the Sicilian Defense is 2)Nf3. This developing move has great influence on the center and serves as the reinforcement for 3)d4. When Black captures the pawn on d4, White will recapture with the knight. White's knight will be beautifully centralized, and Black cannot immediately dislodge this piece without making some serious weaknesses or positional concessions. Of course, Black does not just roll over—instead, it follows the elements! The three main moves on this list are 2)...e6, 2)...Nc6, and 2)...d6. Black's 2)...d6 will be the subject of the next chapter. After 2)Nf3, Black can play 2)...e6 to open a passage to the bishop and a later idea of combating the center with d5 (Diagram 6.8).

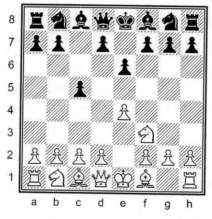

Diagram 6.8: Position after 2)...e6.

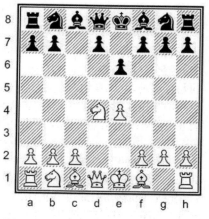

Diagram 6.9: Position after 4)Nxd4.

White's signature move here is 3)d4. This is a very confrontational move gaining space and forcing Black's hand. Black's pawn on c5 is protected, but logical developing moves can send Black's position downward in a hurry. If Black plays 3)...Nf6, it will be chased with 4)e5 Nd5 5)c4, and White already has a huge space advantage. Similarly, if Black played 3)...Nc6, White can play 4)d5 exd5 5)exd5, and Black must move the knight to an undesirable square.

Hmmm. What to do? Black's best choice is to play 3)...cxd4 to release the tension in the center and give the dark-squared bishop extra squares to roam. White plays 4)Nxd4 {Not 4)Qxd4?! Nc6 and Black gains a tempo} and super-centralizes the knight (Diagram 6.9). At this point in time, Black has three to four useful avenues, but there is some crossover (transpositions) between the moves. These can be narrowed to 4)...Nf6 and 4)...a6.

4)...Nf6

In Diagram 6.10, Black plays the developing move 4)...Nf6, attacking the e4 pawn. This is a natural knight move that prevents White from playing the direct move 5)e5 because, after 5)...Qa5+ 6)Nc3 Qxe5+, Black snares the pawn on e5. White should play the patient and element-fitting 5)Nc3 entering the Four Knights of the Sicilian. This also creates a positional threat of 6)e5 demoting the knight on f6 of its duties. In response to White's motives, Black plays 5)...Nc6 to hold down this e5 square. The only move is not 5)...Nc6 (Diagram 6.11). Black can transpose into the Scheveningen Variation of the Sicilian Defense with 5)...d6 to guard the e5 square. The most popular move order is 1)e4 c5 2)Nf3 d6 3)d4 cxd4 4)Nxd4 Nf6 5)Nc3 e6. But we will not cover this variation since it has been put under a cloud from 6)g4!.

I would feel guilty if I did not mention 5)...Bb4 as a plausible move. I have seen this move played multiple times at the amateur level, but it often leaves Black in agony. On the surface it follows the elements, but doesn't it neglect the e5 square? White can displace Black's knight on f6 with 6)e5. Black should play 6)...Nd5, and then the game should unwind 7)Bd2 Nxc3 8)bxc3. If Black retreats by 8)...Be7 or 8)...Ba5, White will play 9)Qg4!. Again, Black is faced with poor choices. Black can try 9)...Kf8, protecting the g7 pawn, but will lose castling privileges. If Black unassumingly plays 9)...0-0 in an attempt to "castle without a hassle," White will rock Black's world by playing 10)Bh6.

Diagram 6.10: Position after 4)...Nf6.

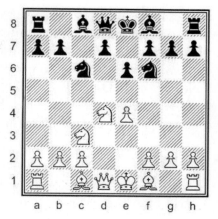

Diagram 6.11: Position after 5)...Nc6.

Black must defend checkmate with 10)...g6, handing over the *exchange* to 11)Bxf8.

The position in Diagram 6.15 typically arises from the move order 1)e4 c5 2)Nf3 e6 3)d4 cxd4 4)Nxd4 Nc6 5)Nc3 Nf6.

Black challenges White's well-stationed knight on d4, and if White does not trade knights, this will help Black control e5 because the knight remains on c6. White is not willing to let Black have it easy, so White plays 6)Nxc6 and Black makes the necessary move 6)...bxc6 {6)...dxc6 7)Qxd8 Kxd8 and Black can no longer castle} to preserve castling rights. After 6)...bxc6, a sample line runs 7)e5 Nd5 8)Ne4 Qc7 {forcing White to weaken the a7 to g1 diagonal to protect the pawn} 9)f4 Qa5+ {9)...Qb6 is a line, but not one I could suggest to play from either side to learn openings} 10)c3 Ba6. White retains some space edge in these lines, but Black is okay.

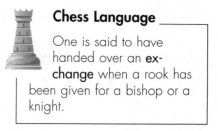

Chess Language

One is said to have handed over an **exchange** when a rook has been given for a bishop or a knight.

4)...a6

Black moves 4)...a6 (the Kan Variation) to adopt a wait-and-see approach, losing time in the process. It keeps out a knight from b5 and can serve as support for the b5 move gaining space on the queenside. Black can set up a very solid position, making it hard for White to move(s) to force the queen from that menacing center that takes up so much space. Black plays the useful developing and attacking move 4)...Nf6 (Diagram 6.13).

One of the key ideas is that if White wants to play e5, he must capture the knight on c6. For example, 5)Nxc6 bxc6, but White cannot play 6)e5 due to Qa5+, and White's ambitions are extinguished. Instead, White plays the precise 5)Nc3 with a huge positional threat of Nxc6 followed by e5, and the knight on f6 has to return its starting square. After 5)Nc3, we have truly reached the crossroads. Black can play 5)... e6 and transpose into the Four Knights of the Sicilian or play 5)...d6 and find himself in a Classical Sicilian. Also, Black can play the interesting move 5)...e5, known as the Sveshnikov (Diagram 6.14).

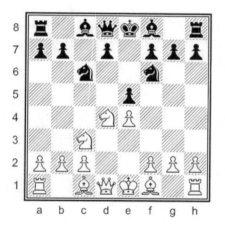

Diagram 6.14: Position after 5)...e5.

Black's goal of 5)...e5 is to bully the knight on d4 and hope it goes to a poor square. It also releases the bishop on f8 from prison. However, it results in a backward d-pawn for Black and a very soft d6 square. White's move to try for an edge relies on the move 6)Ndb5, which is en route to d6. White can't expect to gain any advantage after 6)Nxc6 bxc6 7)Bc4 Bb4. Then what should Black play against 6)Ndb5 with the positional threat of 7)Nd6+? Black cannot secure the square by pieces; rather, it uses the pawn move 6)...d6 to shut down White's idea. White plays 7)Bg5, a normal developing move. Next Black begins to attack White's knight with 7)...a6, and White responds with 8)Na3—the only move for the White knight (Diagram 6.15).

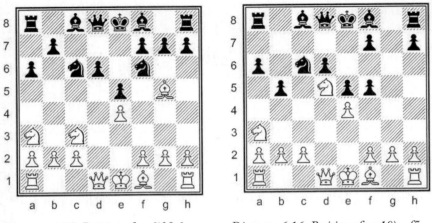

Diagram 6.15: Position after 8)Na3.   *Diagram 6.16: Position after 10)...f5.*

Black makes the natural progression and plays 8)...b5, threatening to play b4 and fork White's knights. This move grabs space on the queenside and gives an additional diagonal for the bishop on c8. This pawn also prevents the knight on a3 rerouting to c4. White diverts Black's attention with the move 9)Bxf6 causing Black to lose a tempo if 9)...Qxf6 and then 10)Nd5 targeting the queen. As a result, Black plays 9)...gxf6, temporarily conceding to doubled f-pawns. White must not forget Black is still pressing to play b4 forking the knights on a3 and c3. White evades the threat and plays 10)Nd5, posting the knight magnificently in the center. Then Black plays 10)...f5 to undouble the pawns (Diagram 6.16). The middlegame war begins ....

The Least You Need to Know

- ◆ The Sicilian is played by the best players in the world.
- ◆ Don't just copy moves: understand the ideas!
- ◆ You must play actively to challenge the Sicilian.
- ◆ Don't let your guard down in the Sicilian minefield.

7

Sicilianaires

In This Chapter

- ◆ The popular Sicilian
- ◆ The Classical
- ◆ Dragons do exist
- ◆ The unwavering Najdorf

As you have read in Chapter 6, there are multiple roads you can take in the Sicilian. We looked at some popular lines after 1)e4 c5 2)Nf3, but none compares to the wealth of Black's second move 2)...d6 (Diagram 7.1). Why is 2)...d6 so special? It helps to develop a piece, and it keeps sight of the e5 square. Black would like to play Nf6 without permitting White to play e5, which would shove the knight on f6 out of the way. If White plays 3)e5? now, Black can capture the pawn with no worries. White can also try 3)Bb5+ (The Moscow), appearing to develop for free, but Black can respond by playing 3)...Bd7, interposing the check. A sample continuation of natural moves is 4)Bxd7+ Nxd7 5)0-0 Ngf6 6)Nc3 g6 7)d4 cxd4 8)Nxd4 Bg7 9)Be3 0-0, and the position is very solid for both sides. This is fine, but White can strive for more ambitious variations to make life harder for Black. What is White's first step toward these hopes?

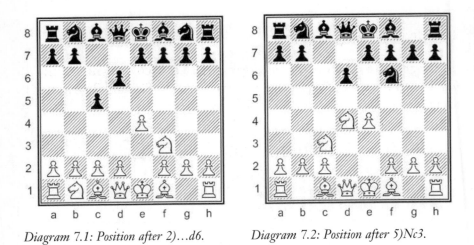

Diagram 7.1: Position after 2)...d6. Diagram 7.2: Position after 5)Nc3.

Remember that in Chapter 6 we discussed "The Move" against the Sicilian Defense. The same move applies now. White should play the active, aggressive, and element-aware 3)d4 ("The Move"). This pawn advance opens up the last bishop and, of course, battles for land in the center. Also, White would like to take the pawn on c5, and if Black recaptures with the pawn on d6 (dxc5), White will play Qxd8+, ruining any chances for Black to castle. With that in mind, Black's most reliable move is 3)...cxd4, liquidating the central pawn. Here White plays the obvious 4)Nxd4, taking over space in the center. A rare sideline is 4)Qxd4 Nc6 5)Bb5 Bd7, when White must part with the light-squared bishop or move the queen from harm's way, but this wastes time. So after 4)Nxd4, Black plays 4)...Nf6, activating the knight and seeking to destroy the pawn on e4. The most logical and effective response is 5)Nc3, developing and defending (Diagram 7.2).

Diagram 7.2 is by far the most frequently reached position within all the variations of the Sicilian. I will call it "The Position" in the Sicilian. Now Black has to make a decision: Black could try the less popular 5)... Nc6, the semipopular 5)...g6 (Dragon), or enter the highly fashionable 5)...a6 (Najdorf). You will be given insight on these variations within the Sicilian Defense and realize that they all follow at least one of the elements. Then you can play the Sicilian comfortably.

Classical Sicilian

In Diagram 7.3, Black plays the very natural 5)...Nc6, helping to contend for the center. This is known as the Classical Sicilian. The one drawback is that it does not help Black castle any faster.

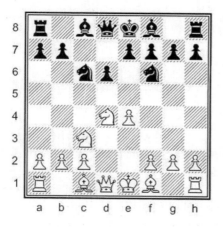

Diagram 7.3: Position after 5)...Nc6.

White could opt for 6)Nxc6, but after 6)...bxc6 Black will have control over the d5 square. I believe the most critical move is 6)Bg5. The intention of this move is to play Bxf6 and force Black to form doubled pawns after either pawn recapture. It would be silly and a waste of time to relocate the knight on f6 elsewhere; rather, it is more logical to play 6)...e6 to be able to meet 7)Bxf6 with 7)...Qxf6, maintaining the pawn structure. Instead, White changes gears with 7)Qd2, preparing to castle queenside. In this particular line, White builds up pressure on Black's d6 pawn with the queen on d2 and eventually with rook on a1 when it reaches d1. On top of that, White sometimes places a menacing knight on b5 to attack the pawn on d6. That is why Black plays the preventative 7)...a6 to keep that knight out, indirectly protecting the d6 pawn. This short pawn move can also help Black to play b5, assisting the march forward on the queenside.

Diagram 7.4: Position after
8)0-0-0.

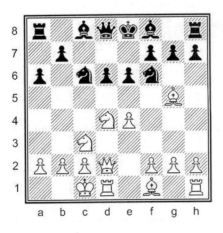

After 6)Bg5 e6 7)Qd2 a6, White plays 8)0-0-0, tucking the king away (Diagram 7.4). Not to be forgotten, the rook is transferred to d1 with an *x-ray* on Black's d6 pawn. Black has a few playable moves here. Black could follow the main move 8)...Bd7 and the game could continue 9)f4 b5 10)Bxf6 gxf6. White may have a slight advantage because of a plus in time and space, but Black has the bishop pair, and Black's king is not so easily attacked behind the wall of pawns. Black has doubled pawns, but what if Black had kept the pawn intact with 10)...Qxf6?

The capture is risky after 11)e5 dxe5 12)Ndxb5, threatening Qxd7 checkmate. Black defends with 12)...Qd8 13)Nd6+ Bxd6 14)Qxd6, and Black is worse due to the position of the king.

When White plays 8)0-0-0 in Diagram 7.4, Black can also try 8)...Be7. The next few moves are 9)Nxc6 {9)f4 is more accurate} bxc6 10)Bxf6 gxf6 (Diagram 7.5). Although Black is given double pawns, White has to get rid of the centralized knight on d4. I believe the position is

Chess Language

An **x-ray** is when a piece can see through other pieces and exists on the same file, rank, or diagonal. This means that even if a piece cannot directly go to a square, it still has a presence and an indirect effect on that square.

unclear, but I would prefer to play Black. White retains a better pawn structure and has a small lead in time. However, Black has the bishop pair and can utilize the b-file. Black has the idea of Rb8 and Qb6 creating threats against White's king. Also, Black can time the d5 pawn thrust, gaining more space in the center. In contrast, White has no concrete plan.

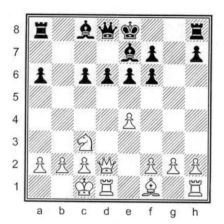

Diagram 7.5: Position after 10)...gxf6.

The Sicilian Dragon: Love and Hate

The Sicilian Dragon is named after the constellation Draco (dragon), which resembles the pawn structure of this opening. Known for fancy sacrifices and unimaginable combinations, the name fits well. The game is usually defined by a race to the opponent's king. Whoever reaches the opponent's king first wins. As a faithful dragoneer for about a decade, I have truly enjoyed exercising my brain in these cliffhanger positions. It is an extremely fun line to play, but above the master level it is hard to be regularly successful with this line against a ready opponent. (I will explain this later.) Don't be fooled, though; it is very sharp and a good weapon, particularly at the amateur levels. The Dragon ignites with 5)...g6 (Diagram 7.6). I believe that you know the primary reason why this follows the principles. Okay, I will tell you anyway. This gives the bishop on f8 access to g7, and then Black will be able to castle in short order.

At this juncture, White has so many ways to play. To cover these lines in depth, it would take a series of books the size of this one to truly give the Dragon the justice it deserves. That's why I will stick with 6)Be3, best by test. White has many plans here, but before I move on, I should note that 6)Bc4 follows the elements just as well as 6)Be3. Also, there is the possibility of White transposing into 6)Be3 positions by playing 6)Bc4. White's purpose of Be3 is to castle on the queenside as soon as possible and formulate an attack on the Black's kingside.

Diagram 7.6: Position after
5)...g6.

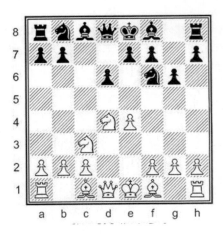

White's 6)Be3 also helps reinforce the knight on d4. Black continues with the simple 6)...Bg7 in the sequence. Logically, White would like to play 7)Qd2 to castle on the next move, but this is an inaccuracy. Now Black can get away with 7)...Ng4, intending to capture the bishop. 8)Bb5+ is met by 8)...Bd7, so White should just move the bishop on e3. Why? If White loses the bishop, the dark squares will become weak, and it will be harder to go after Black's king. Instead, White should try 8)Bg5 {not 8)Bf4? because of 8)...Bxd4 9)Qxd4 e5 winning a piece for Black}. Then, after 8)...h6 9)Bh4 Nc6 10)Bb5 Bd7, Black is doing well.

Let's use simple logic to solve the problem. White would like to play 7)Qd2 but is faced with the annoying 7)...Ng4. It is our job to prevent the knight from trespassing on g4. Both 7)f3 and 7)h3 take care of business by controlling the g4 square. I prefer 7)f3 (this is the main line) because it also supports the central e4 pawn. Also, White usually plays h4 storming Black's king, so White does not want to use the h-pawn to hold the g4 square. The position that results from 7)f3 is called the Yugoslav Attack. Black has two moves that are interchangeable for the most part: 7)...0-0 or 7)...Nc6. Usually, one is played after the other. Black could also enter the newly developed Dragondorf with 7)...a6. It's a hybrid of the Dragon and Najdorf variations. However, we will go with Black's move 7)...0-0. Now White safely plays 8)Qd2, and Black plays the element-oriented 8)...Nc6 (Diagram 7.7).

8)...Nc6 keeps a watchful eye on the e5 square. The black pawn on d6 is no longer needed to oversee e5. Now that Black has castled and is mostly developed, he or she would like to strike in the center. Black aspires to play 9)...d5, prying the position open. It is considered the "equalizer" in the Dragon variation. If Black is allowed to play this move effectively, Black will at least be equal.

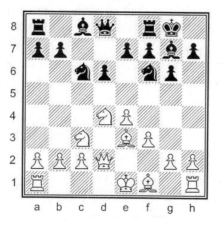

Diagram 7.7: Position after 8)...Nc6.

However, White has two unanimous choices, both aimed at preventing this d5 shot: 9)Bc4 and 9)0-0-0. In Diagram 7.8, White's 9)Bc4 is a direct attempt to stop Black from playing d5. Also, White's last minor piece is developed and now has the freedom of choice to castle on either side. (White typically castles queenside.) Black should answer with the usual move 9)...Bd7.

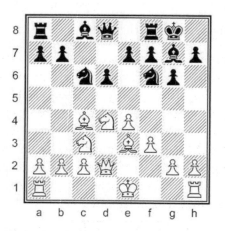

Diagram 7.8: Position after 9)Bc4.

The automatic move after 9)...Bd7 is 10)0-0-0. White has all pieces primed and ready for a full assault on the Black king. All White's minor pieces are well mobilized, and the rooks are connected. I would compare this line to a game of "capture the flag": the first to capture the opponent's flag, or king in this case, will be crowned victorious. White and Black must not lose sight of the objective. Either side can find itself in a predicament if it plays nonchalantly or without a plan.

Black has many plans after 10)0-0-0, and they all involve dethroning the White king as quickly as possible. Moves such as 10)...Rc8, 10)...Qa5, and 10)...Rb8 stick to the program. Over the last decade, with the help of computers, the Dragon variation has gone through a turbulent ride. I believe if White plays accurately, the moves 10)...Rc8 and 10)...Qa5 can lead to some unstable positions for Black. For those wishing to pursue the complications of the Dragon, you must research more. I can, however, suggest to play 10)...Rb8—the Chinese Dragon. Black intends to rip open the b-file, often sacrificing the pawn to gain a very significant initiative. White does not have to comply with these complications, but the game will still be more than playable from Black's perspective. I have had excellent results with the Chinese Dragon, and I definitely feel it's a solid choice against this Yugoslav line.

I would like to discuss White's other ninth move, 9)0-0-0 (seen in Diagram 7.9) instead of 9)Bc4. It indirectly defends against 9)...d5. For example, 10)Nxc6 bxc6 11)exd5 Nxd5 12)Nxd5 cxd5 13)Qxd5 and White nets a pawn. This is a known variation in which Black has some compensation for the lost pawn but hardly more than that. Although this is true, Black is not obligated to play 9)...d5. Moves like 9)...Bd7, 9)...Be6, or 9)...Nxd4 are playable, but I strongly feel that White retains more favorable positions from all of these moves by Black. This is one reason {to avoid 9)0-0-0} why people choose to play the Accelerated Dragon.

Diagram 7.9: Position after
9)0-0-0.

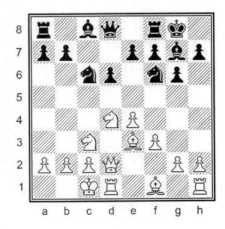

The Accelerated Dragon arises from the move order 1)e4 c5 2)Nf3 Nc6 3)d4 cxd4 4)Nxd4 g6. As you see, Black does not commit the d-pawn early so that the move d5 can be played in one motion. The idea can be seen in the following moves if White tries to transpose into the normal Dragon: 5)Nc3 Bg7 6)Be3 Nf6 7)f3 0-0 8)Qd2. Now Black can play 8)...d6, returning to the normal Dragon line, but it can be avoided by 8)...d5! challenging White in the center. Notice that Black has gained a move. Instead of playing d6 and then d5, Black can play d5 only using one move. Nevertheless, White should play 8)Bc4 to bring the d5 move to a halt. Here, Black plays 8)...d6, transposing into a perfectly playable line for Black while avoiding the 9)0-0-0 line.

So what is the ultimate verdict of the Dragon? It can lead to exciting games and is definitely an opening I can recommend all the way up to the master level. It remains very playable, but the Najdorf has overshadowed the Dragon.

Najdorf

Through thick and thin, Bobby Fischer and Garry Kasparov used the Najdorf (named after the late Grandmaster Miguel Najdorf) as their primary defense for Black against 1)e4. Arguably the two best World Champions played this with great faith, and the world seems to have followed suit. The most popular opening in modern chess begins with 5)...a6 (Diagram 7.10).

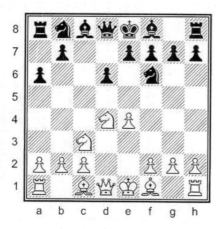

Diagram 7.10: Position after 5)...a6.

What? That's it? A mere pawn move is all the rage? It does not develop a piece, and it only controls one square! Look closer. The a6 move adopts a flexible approach and helps to play b5 expanding on the queenside. In the meantime, it takes away the b5 square from both of White's knights and the bishop on f1. The a6 move may not gain so much space directly, but it takes away critical squares from White. Remember, you can improve your space not only by grabbing your own but by denying squares to your opponent. Many times, Black would like to play e5 to dislocate the white knight on d4. The lack of a6 can be seen if Black were to play 5)...e5 rather than 5)...a6. White can play 6)Bb5+, and after 6)...Bd7 7)Bxd7 Qxd7 8)Nf5, White has a pleasant position. Black's d6 pawn is vulnerable down the line, and White has a vice grip on the d5 square. Black cannot play d5 to free up the position, and this means that White has a space advantage. The less notable move 6)...Nbd7 blocks the bishop on c8, and it relinquishes the f5 square to White's knight. Therefore, a6 agrees with the elements.

There are various responses that White can try, ranging from safe to aggressive. Only a few really put Black's system to a test. White can play the active 6)Bc4, but this has not given Black as many problems compared to 6)Be3 and 6)Bg5. White can play the highly popular approach 6)Be3 (English Attack), but it does not make Black sweat as much as 6)Bg5. I would like to work out the 6)Bg5 line to make sure Black has a pulse.

White wants to develop as quickly as possible, simultaneously creating "threats" in Black's army. White can play 6)Bg5 to exploit Black's setup (Diagram 7.11). White activates a piece while creating the positional threat of Bxf6 when Black must create doubled pawns to recapture the bishop.

Diagram 7.11: Position after 6)Bg5.

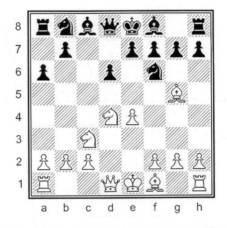

Black does not desire doubled pawns and plays 6)...e6. 7)Bxf6 is harmless because of 7)...Qxf6, and Black's pawn structure is maintained. For half a century, it has been understood that 7)f4 is the thematic move in the position. From an element standpoint, this grabs more space, notably the e5 square. When the black knight on b8 goes to d7 or c6, it would like to head to e5, but this square has been taken away. The pawn on f4 adds another ingredient because White has premonitions of playing e5, attacking Black's knight. Oops. Black cannot move the knight on f6 because that will expose the queen. How does Black react to the disruptive move 7)f4?

Black can play the usual developing move 7)...Be7, considered one of the main lines, but it has lost momentum to 7)...Qb6 (Poisoned Pawn Variation). Despite this, I feel 7)...Be7 is the safer and more solid choice for players at the amateur levels (Diagram 7.12).

Black's move 7)...Be7 relieves this pin on the knight, and it prepares Black to castle. If White tries the straightforward 8)e5, then 8)...dxe5 9)fxe5 Nd5 and Black should not have opening problems. White plays 8)Qf3 in place of 8)e5. White is now ready to castle queenside, and the queen supports the e-pawn. There is also a hidden idea behind 8)Qf3. If Black plays the unassuming 8)...b5?, White will play 9)e5!, attacking the knight on f6 and the rook on a8 with the queen. Black will not necessarily lose a piece, but some material will be lost. The complications favor White.

Diagram 7.12: Position after 7)...Be7.

Diagram 7.13: Position after 10)...b5.

The best-known move for Black after 8)Qf3 is 8)...Qc7. This move serves two purposes. First, it prevents the bishop on f1 from going to the active c4 square. It also helps to play b5 because when White plays e5, Black can play the intermezzo Bb7, attacking the White queen. As you would expect, White plays 9)0-0-0. I know that I told you that Qc7 helps to play b5, but the immediate 9)...b5 may not be so accurate. A sample line runs 10)e5 Bb7 11)Qg3 protecting e5, and White's e5 pawn is a real thorn in Black's position. So Black plays 9)...Nbd7 to add reinforcements to the e5 square first. Next White moves forward with 10)g4, and now Black continues 10)...b5, staking out space on the queenside (Diagram 7.13).

We have reached a position that in many ways was turned into the main line by Bobby Fischer. White cannot play 11)e5 because Black plays 11)...Bb7. The White queen must move, and then Black will take the rook on h1, winning material and rudely awakening White. Ultimately, both sides have reached a playable position in Diagram 7.13. Now the real war begins.

Both sides have survived the opening, but the Najdorf is hardly a line to let your guard down. If you play either side of this opening, especially from Black's perspective, I recommend that you research games with 6)Bc4, 6)Be3, and 6)Bg5 to get a better understanding of these very complex positions.

The Least You Need to Know

♦ If you need to win, the main Sicilian is a great weapon.

♦ Have faith in the Sicilian but don't relax.

♦ The Dragon is fun to play.

♦ Of all the Sicilian variations, the Najdorf may be the most sound.

Chapter 8

The Narrow, French, and Caro

In This Chapter

- ◆ The hypermodern openings
- ◆ Interesting but questionable
- ◆ The reputable and recognized

By now, you should have a good feel for the purpose of 1)e4. As we've seen, Black can play the most popular 1)...e5 or 1)...c5, but are those the only good moves? This has always been a debate. Should Black attempt to fight for the center (space) from the first move of the game {1)...e5}, or should Black try to control it from a distance {1)...c5}? The legends and champions of chess have almost always advocated the importance of central play. The question with the *hypermodern* approaches is that they tend to give White too much space, particularly in the center. With less space it is more difficult to coordinate and mobilize your pieces in the opening.

We will inspect these hypermodern ideas in the opening, and we will use the elements to see why these openings are not so popular among the best players in the world. You will see that only some of these openings can be played with faith. The Sicilian Defense, which we have already seen, is an example of a hypermodern defense that offers good chances for Black. Although the pieces do not occupy the center squares, they fight for the center through the high activity of the minor pieces.

The Narrow

Against the formidable 1)e4, players have attempted 1)...b6 and 1)...a6. These first moves for Black are very questionable because they concede the entire center. White usually follows up with 2)d4, gaining the classic center. Here, White either controls or occupies all four central squares. Black is not following the elements and is being too submissive. Don't get me wrong, these lines are not outright losing, but they certainly will not guarantee you a playable position. Against strong opposition, playing moves such as 1)...b6 or 1)...a6 can spell doom. These are bad habits that you should stay away from!

Alekhine Defense: 1)...Nf6

If there were one weakness to expose from the move 1)e4, it is the fact that this pawn is unprotected. Why not attack this pawn? Black plays 1)...Nf6, developing a piece and provoking the e-pawn to move forward, further away from its own army (Diagram 8.1). The knight move makes sense, but White can try to attack this knight with tempi while taking over space.

Diagram 8.1: Position after 1)...Nf6.

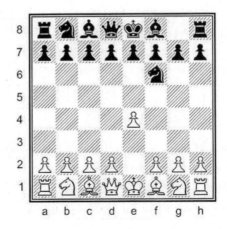

The challenging move for Black to meet is 2)e5 putting a question to the knight on f6. Black's only adequate move is 2)...Nd5. This knight is a lone soldier, and White can hunt down the knight by playing 3)c4 Nb6 4)c5 Nd5 5)Bc4 e6, but I think White *overextends* the pawns. I believe the quiet move 3)d4 pays attention to the elements, and it can result in a space advantage generating an overall better position. Black's main response is 3)...d6 to undermine White's center and free the bishop. White sends another pawn Black's way with 4)c4, and then Black has only one safe move for the knight in 4)...Nb6. {4)...Nb4 5)Qa4+ N4c6 6)d5 and White wins a piece.}

Chess Language

As opposed to the classical 1)...e5, **hypermodern** openings are concerned with controlling the center with pieces rather than occupying the central squares: d4, d5, e4, and e5. When a chess player says a position has been **overextended,** this means that the army has gone too far. More territory may be overtaken, but as a result the soldiers are easily attacked or pushed back.

In this position, Black would like to trade pawns on e5 and then play Qxd1+, no longer allowing White to castle. White could prevent this idea and launch the four pawns attack with 5)f4, but it lacks development. I cannot teach bad habits like this! The modest 5)exd6 does the trick. Black usually plays 5)...exd6 or 5)...cxd6 to regain the pawn. {5)...Qxd6 6)c5 and Black loses a piece.} Black's 5)...exd6 provides a square for the bishop on f8 (Diagram 8.2).

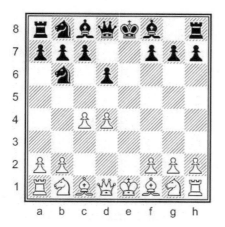

Diagram 8.2: Position after 5)...exd6.

crack. However, this is not a line that fully satisfies elements because Black will fall behind in development. 4)...a6 can also be played if Black wants to maintain the chance of transposing into the Najdorf Variation of the Sicilian Defense. A sample of a line in the Kan after 4)...a6 is 5)Nc3 b5 6)Bd3 Qb6 7)Nb3 Qc7 8)0-0 Bb7 9)Qe2 d6 10)f4 Nd7 11)Bd2 Ngf6 12)Rael Be7 and White has the initiative due to the central presence and piece placement. Black may do better with 8)...Nf6 9)f4 b4.

2)...Nc6

A perfect move in terms of following the elements is 2)...Nc6, except Black will not be able to castle as quickly (Diagram 6.12). It activates a piece to control central squares d4 and e5, highlighting a very important point: when Black plays Nf6, it is ideal to not allow White to play e5, harassing the knight on f6. If White is given permission to do so, Black's knight will be driven back, and critical space will lost. These ideas will be more evident in the next few main moves.

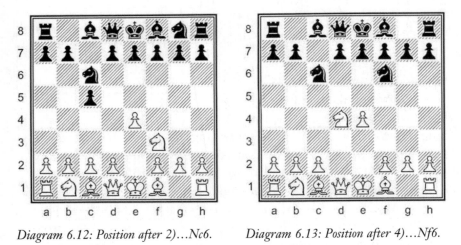

Diagram 6.12: Position after 2)...Nc6.   *Diagram 6.13: Position after 4)...Nf6.*

As expected, the most principled move is 3)d4. White lashes out in the center, opens a line for the bishop on c1, and the queen has a presence on its starting square. Black's most effective move is the simple 3)...cxd4, and White makes the logical move 4)Nxd4 centralizing the knight. Black would love to trade knights by playing 4)...Nxd4, but after 5)Qxd4, White's queen will be favorably placed in the middle of the board. The ultimate problem for Black is that there is no effective

The game continues with the natural moves 6)Nc3 Be7. This is where White needs to move precisely for a positional edge. 7)Nf3 lets Black have a good square for the bishop and pin the white knight with 7)...Bg4. In these variations, the best square for the knight is usually e2. However, White should not play 7)Nge2 yet because that blocks the f1 bishop. That means White should play 7)Bd3 and only then play Nge2, granting the pieces harmony. Next Black plays the developing 7)...Nc6, and White responds with 8)Nge2, defending d4 and activating a piece. When Black plays 8)...Bg4, White can play 9)f3, releasing the pin with a tempo. Black will play 9)...Bh5 to retreat the bishop, and then both sides will castle 10)0-0 0-0 (Diagram 8.3).

Diagram 8.3: Position after 10)...0-0.

Black's position may be in no real danger, but it is annoying because it is hard to produce an effective plan. White controls more space than Black, making it especially difficult to maneuver the pieces. The Black bishop on e7 plays a passive role, and the knight on b6 appears to have no immediate future. These reasons lead me to believe that White is better, and this is probably not the best opening to use from Black's perspective.

Center Stage

On the first move of the game, Black can challenge White's center with 1)...d5, known as the Center-Counter Game or Scandinavian (Diagram 8.4). This move appears to be on the good side of the elements as it opens up the bishop on c8 and it bursts in the center. White plays 2)exd5 and does not hesitate to liquidate the pawn. The other

point is that if Black continues 2)...Qxd5, White plays 3)Nc3, attacking
the queen with a tempo. Despite this, this variation has gained some
momentum, particularly with 3)...Qd6. This is an odd square for the
queen, but it cannot be disturbed so easily. Of course, White could play
4)Ne4 or 4)Nb5, but Black could transfer the queen to safety at no cost.
White's game is enhanced by playing the simple 4)d4, conquering more
territory. From here, a logical continuation is 4)...Nf6 5)Nf3 a6 6)Bd3
Bg4 7)h3 Bh5 8)0-0 Nc6 9)Ne4 Nxe4 10)Bxe4 e6 11)c3, and White has
a slight plus in space and a preferable position.

It should be noted that 3)...Qa5 is the most common move after 3)Nc3.
However, Alexei Shirov (ranked as high as number four in the world)
has come up with ideas that have set Black some difficulties in this line.
The variation continues 4)d4 Nf6 5)Nf3 c6—creating an escape route
for the queen—6)Bc4 Bf5 7)Bd2 e6 8)Nd5 Qd8 9)Nxf6+ Qxf6 10)Qe2
Nd7 {10)...Bxc2?! is too greedy; for example, the usefulness of Qe2 is
revealed with 11)d5! cxd5 12)Bxd5 Qe7 13)Qb5+ Qd7 14)Qxb7 Qxd5
15)Qc8+ Qd8 16)Qxc2 Be7 17)0-0 0-0 18)Rfd1 and White has the
upper hand} 11)0-0-0. White's space and piece activity secure a definite
positional advantage. For more analysis, visit willthethrillaramil.com.

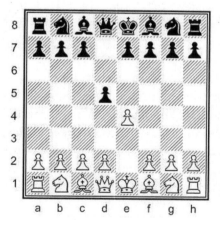

Diagram 8.4: Position after
1)...d5.

French Fighters?!

In a correspondence match between clubs from London and Paris in
1834, Paris triumphed in this opening position. Thereafter, it has been
recognized as the French.

The French has the reputation of being a tough nut to crack, but how many cracks does it take to get to the center of the nut? The French is characterized by a solid pawn structure, but it surrenders space. The overall hope of this opening is that White will leave weaknesses when attacking, and when the attack fails, Black will have a superior end-game. I guess you could call it a "rope-a-dope" opening. In some cases, Black will expand on the queenside while White gains ground on the kingside. The seemingly cowardly French Defense begins with 1)...e6 (Diagram 8.5).

Diagram 8.5: Position after 1)...e6.

This modest pawn move controls d5 and supplies a diagonal to the bishop on f8. White plays 2)d4 and says, "Thank you for the center." Black says, "Hold that thought," and continues 2)...d5 to struggle for the middle of the board. Black is also threatening White's e4 pawn. White can play 3)exd5, but after 3)...exd5 the position is symmetrical, and both sides share the same benefits. White has more critical attempts to break down Black's fortress.

Advance Variation

In this line, White locks the position up, hoping to cramp and immobilize Black. White commences the action with 3)e5. This guards the squares d6 and f6 deep in Black's camp. Most importantly, this takes away the natural f6 square for the knight on g8. The only thing protecting the pawn on e5 is the pawn on d4. Therefore, Black attacks the base (d4) of the pawn chain with 3)...c5. White plays 4)c3, defending the base, and Black continues 4)...Nc6, building additional pressure on d4. Notice that if Black had played Nc6 before c5, it would have blocked the c-pawn. That is why c5 is played first.

The constant focal point in this position is d4. If Black can manage to win this pawn harmlessly or force White into awkward defenses, then Black's opening is usually a success. White plays 5)Nf3 to solidify the central d4 and e5 pawns, and Black brings another friend to the fight with 5)...Qb6 (Diagram 8.6).

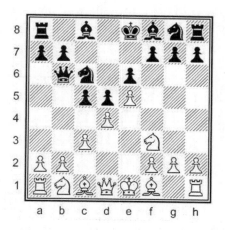

Diagram 8.6: Position after 5)...Qb6.

The key aspects of Qb6 rely on placing more strain on d4 while holding back the White bishop on c1. If this bishop were to move, Black could play Qxb2, winning a pawn, severely disturbing White's queenside. White does not want this bishop on c1 to become just a defender and plays 6)a3. How in the world does this help develop the bishop?

This will support the move b4; in turn, this will provide the b2 square for the bishop. Remember the focus. Black plays 6)...Nh6 to head to the f5 square. White would like to play 7)Bxh6, but Black can respond with the intermezzo 7)...Qxb2. Instead, White plays 7)b4, making use of the a3 pawn. One road that can be taken is 7)...cxd4 8)cxd4 {8)Bxh6 gxh6 9)cxd4 is also playable} Nf5 9)Bb2 Bd7 10)g4 Nfe7. Who is really better here? White has a space advantage, but the pawns have been pushed a bit far and can become a liability later on. I would assess this position as being unclear. The Advance Variation is interesting but is probably not the best antidote for the French Defense.

A Knightmare

In the sequence 1)e4 e6 2)d4 d5, White should not feel obligated to move the pawn on e4. White has two knight moves: 3)Nc3 and Nd2, which defend the e-pawn. I am not a big fan of 3)Nc3 because it allows Black to play 3)...Bb4 (The Winawer), pinning the knight. For White to hold on to the pawn, Black is given the freedom to play Bxc3+, creating doubled pawns in White's position. Despite this negative aspect, this line is currently creating difficulties for Black because White will have extra space and the bishop pair to boot. Overall, too much theoretical knowledge is required. For simplicity and effectiveness, I will give the nod to 3)Nd2, the Tarrasch (Diagram 8.7).

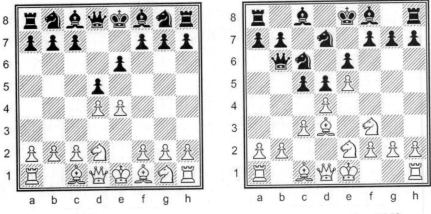

Diagram 8.7: Position after 3)Nd2.   *Diagram 8.8: Position after 8)Nf3.*

If Black plays 3)...Bb4 now, White will play 4)c3, kicking the bishop back. Another idea is that after 3)...dxe4, the White knight will be better placed after 4)Nxe4. (These lines are playable for Black.) Black's French move is 3)...Nf6. White basically takes space in the center while Black organizes the pieces to counter against this center. For example, the line runs 4)e5 redirecting the knight, and Black plays 4)...Nfd7. The game continues 5)Bd3 c5 6)c3 Nc6 7)Ne2, a sophisticated knight move. The idea is to let the other knight on d2 go to the f3 square. This will allow both knights to provide backup to the pawn on d4, further cementing the center. Then the moves are 7)...Qb6 8)Nf3 (Diagram 8.8).

Black's position is solid, but it lacks a bit of space. To open up the doors, Black plays 8)...cxd4 when White plays 9)cxd4 to save the pawn. Now Black could play 9)...Bb4+, but this only helps White's cause. White will play 10)Bd2 and possibly trade this White bishop that is difficult to effectively develop in the French. Black typically plays 9)...f6 to soften up White's strongpoint. White is essentially forced to play 10)exf6, and Black activates the knight with 10)...Nxf6. Finally, White plays 11)0-0 and Black develops with 11)...Bd6.

At this point, Black has achieved a fair share of territory in the center. For Black to free up the position, a backward pawn was created on e6. It is not an immediate problem, but if Black does not accurately handle the position, it can be a thorn. White usually plays b3 and then Bb2 to restrict Black from breaking through with e5. White seems to a have a tiny advantage, but the fight has just begun.

Caro-Kann

The Caro-Kann Defense can be compared to a driver's education teacher who always teaches safety first. The variations we are going to look at are merely the keys to the car in the Caro-Kann Defense. You must pay attention and remember the principles. White is going to try to make Black swerve off the road. Be careful! The Caro-Kann Defense begins with 1)e4 c6 (Diagram 8.9). Any questions?

In case you were curious about how this opening acquired its quirky name, it is a combination of the names Horatio Caro and Marcus Kann, who published analysis on this position.

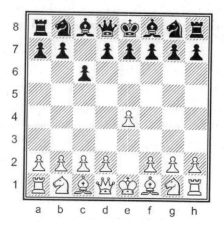

Diagram 8.9: Position after 1)...c6.

We already learned that 1)e4 is a good move because it follows the elements, but Black has a more reserved approach in mind. 1)...c6 does not gain space or open up pathways to the bishops. On top of that, it takes away the most natural square (c6) from the knight. Why would world-class players like Karpov do such a thing? Well, the former World Champion Karpov could see in the future and realize that the pawn advance 2)...d5 would be a good move to counter in the center. If you take a look, 1)...c6 is a useful move to prepare this pawn advance 2)...d5. In response to 1)...c6, White plays 2)d4, grabbing the classic center. Black responds 2)...d5 in accordance with the elements.

The Advance

As in the French Defense, White can play 3)e5 to take away squares from Black (Diagram 8.10). 3)e5 gains more space in the center while denying the g8 knight its natural square f6. Black intends to play e6 to give the bishop on f8 a diagonal, but that would lock in the bishop on c8. Before this is done, Black plays 3)...Bf5, developing toward the center. White can play 4)Bd3, challenging Black's bishop in the center, and prepare for rapid castling. There are other logical moves such as 4)Nc3 that are more complicated, but offer greater chances for an advantage.

When White plays 4)Bd3, Black plays 4)...Bxd3 to avoid wasting time retreating the bishop. Besides, the Black bishop cannot retreat to any adequate squares. White plays 5)Qxd3 and Black follows with 5)...e6, supporting d5 and providing the bishop on f8 a useful diagonal. The game continues 6)Nc3 Qb6, putting pressure on the d4 and b2 pawns. The queen move also aims to keep White from developing the bishop on c1 for a few moves. White plays 7)Nge2 to support the d4 pawn, but White also plans to castle and play f4 to storm the king side. Black can react with 7)...c5, returning the c6 square to the knight and putting more pressure on the d4 pawn.

In the next few moves, both sides will castle. Black will try to expand in the center and on the queenside where Black's pawn chain f7 to d5 aims. White will advance on the kingside and center where White has the most space.

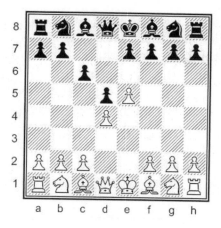

Diagram 8.10: Position after 3)e5.

Main Line

White does not have to touch the pawn on e4 and can play 3)Nc3. Unlike the French, there is no bishop to pin this knight. Black should relieve the tension and play 3)...dxe4. White recaptures by playing 4)Nxe4 (Diagram 8.11). We have entered the main highway of the Caro-Kann.

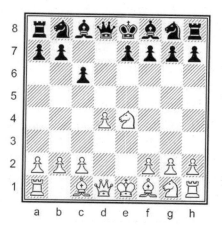

Diagram 8.11: Position after 4)Nxe4.

White now has his or her knight placed in the center of the board where it attacks the most squares, and it has eliminated Black's only central pawn. Black desires to activate the knight with 4)...Nf6, but after 5)Nxf6 exf6 Black's pawn structure is damaged. Black plays 4)...Nd7 to prepare 5)...Ngf6. White has a few options here, but 5)Ng5 forces Black to play with accuracy to sidestep unwanted positions.

The best move is considered 5)Ng5, targeting the f7 square aiming to attack the king. The game follows with 5)...Ngf6 6)Bc4, developing while threatening the f7 square. Black blocks this diagonal with 6)...e6. This move locks in the c8 bishop, but the pressure on f7 must be relieved because king safety takes priority. 7)Qe2 is White's next move, pressuring the e6 pawn and concocting the tactical idea 8)Nxf7 Kxf7 followed by 9)Qxe6+. For example, if Black plays the unassuming 7)...Be7 planning to castle, White will respond with the powerful 8)Nxf7. Then Black is practically forced to play 8)...Kxf7. Finally, the game will end fatally for Black after 9)Qxe6+ Kg6 10)Bd3+ Kh5 11)Qh3 checkmate.

To avoid the same fate, Black should play the aware 7)...Nb6, hoping to swap the knight for the bishop on c4 while protecting the e6 pawn with the c8 bishop. A few natural moves are 8)Bd3 and then 8)...h6, driving away the dangerous knight. A possible series of moves is 9)N5f3 c5 10)dxc5 Bxc5 11)Ne5 Nbd7 12)Ngf3 Qc7 13)0-0 0-0. White started by attacking Black early to gain a slight lead in development. Since then, Black has successfully fended off the attack and safely tucked away the king. Now both sides are ready to duke it out in the middlegame.

The Least You Need to Know

- The Narrow is not as popular as other defenses for a reason.
- Be prepared to have a bit less space when using hypermodern defenses.
- Playing hypermodern defenses requires accuracy; otherwise you can find yourself pushed in a corner real quick.
- The French and Caro-Kann are some of the more reliable alternatives to 1)...e5 or the Sicilian Defense.

1)d4 Openings

We have seen the powerful effects of White's 1)e4, but surely there are other reasonable first moves for White. If White does not play 1)e4, that usually means White will go for 1)d4. It follows the elements in almost the exact same way. However, the positions usually end up completely different. 1)e4 positions are often open positions with much more mobility for each side, while 1)d4 tends to lead to more closed positions.

These closed positions translate into more subtle maneuvers, which make realizing the effects of the elements more unclear. I will make this much more clear and understandable through specific moves and analysis. In the end, these moves will use the elements to arrive at a playable position. Then you will be ready to clash in 1)d4 openings.

Chapter 9

1)d4 d5

In This Chapter

- ◆ The d-pawn meets d-pawn
- ◆ Queen's Gambit
- ◆ The Slav formation

You may have the impression that 1)e4 is the only good way to begin a game of chess. Not so fast! There is another move that is in harmony with the elements. What other move grants you the road to the center and allows teammates to access the battlefield? 1)d4 is that move. 1)d4 echoes the elements like 1)e4, except it does not allow you to castle as quick. However, the advantage it holds over 1)e4 is that the d-pawn is already protected by the queen on d1. That means the pawn is not subject to attack on the first move of the game, as in the Alekhine Defense {1)e4 Nf6}.

As we know, 1)d4 follows the elements, and logically it is still played by the best chess players. It was even the trademark for the former World Champion Mikhail Botvinnik. This move also rubbed off on Garry Kasparov, the most dominant player of his generation. Unfortunately, 1)d4 has the reputation of leading into more positional and quiet games. Don't expect a quick knockout for either side, but 1)d4 can be a powerful weapon, and it should not be taken lightly. Let's not forget, White threatens to play 2)e4, building a classic center. If Black allows this, then White will transpose back into 1)e4 positions with pawns on e4 and d4.

When it comes to the first moves, 1)e4 and 1)d4 are the two main routes taken by the majority of chess players. In this chapter, you will feel the presence of 1)d4 and realize the strangulating effects it can have on an opponent. If Black does not play assertively, White will monopolize the territory on the board and eventually overtake Black's army. You will understand how to pressure Black with 1)d4 and also learn to defend well against this first move of White with 1)...d5. We will apply the elements to mobilize our forces and reach a suitable opening from either side of the board after 1)d4 d5 (Diagram 9.1).

Diagram 9.1: Position after 1)...d5.

Queen's Gambit

When White plays 1)d4, Black should not allow White to play 2)e4, taking over the central squares. What better way to replicate 1)d4 than 1)...d5. Black rightfully takes an equal share of the center while providing squares for the queen and bishop like White. How does White break this equilibrium in the position?

White can play simple developing moves such as 2)Nf3 or 2)Nc3, but these moves have no immediate threat on Black's position. The elements can be followed with 2)c4, creating an imbalance (Diagram 9.2).

White seeks to destroy Black's only central pawn to grab more space. At this point, Black can accept this "gift" or humbly decline the invitation.

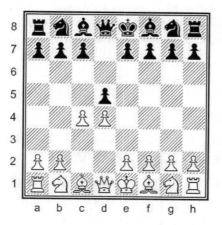

Diagram 9.2: Position after 2)c4.

I Accept!

Isn't White just losing a pawn? Black has to "see it to believe it" and so plays 2)...dxc4 (Diagram 9.3). Black wins a pawn, but Black moves the d-pawn from the center and forms doubled c-pawns. White plays 3)e4 because Black no longer holds down the e4 square. This aggressive pawn move allows White to pose in the center and frees the bishop to attack the pawn on c4.

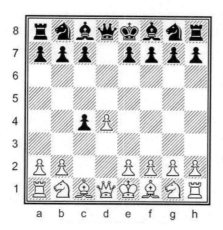

Diagram 9.3: Position after 2)...dxc4.

White definitely has an intimidating center, but Black must not let White develop as he or she pleases. Black can try to undermine White's center with 3)...e5 when the normal response is 4)Nf3 {4)dxe5 Qxd1+ 5)Kxd1 b5 and Black has no difficulties}. There is no rush to capture the Black pawn on c4. Instead, White prefers time and space. The only sound choice for Black is 4)...exd4. Now White gobbles the c4 pawn with 5)Bxc4, preparing to castle (Diagram 9.4). Black is up a pawn, but White already has two pieces mobilized, and the king will be tucked away shortly. Also, White can win the pawn back on d4 if it is not defended.

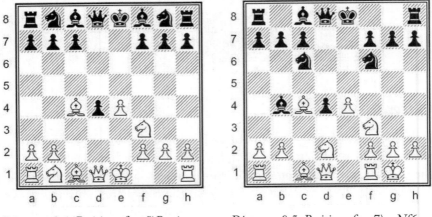

Diagram 9.4: Position after 5)Bxc4.   Diagram 9.5: Position after 7)...Nf6.

Should Black protect the pawn or just give it back to gain time? One of Black's disruptive moves is 5)...Bb4+. A piece is brought into the game with a tempo, and when the check is blocked with 6)Nbd2, the White queen will be cut off from assisting in attacking the d4 pawn. Black calls out another piece to the middle of the battlefield with 6)...Nc6. The pawn on d4 has an extra guard now. White would like to play Nb3 to triple-attack the pawn on d4, but the bishop on b4 pins the knight on d2. To carry out this plan, White must play 7)0-0 first. In Diagram 9.5, Black plays 7)...Nf6 to hold back White's plan of 8)Nb3 gaining back the material.

If 8)Nb3, Black can play the bold and risky 8)...Nxe4 but taking the pawn on e4 may be more trouble than it's worth. Black should play 8)...0-0 with a fine position.

Let's start from Diagram 9.5 again. Before White gives Black the chance to castle, White plays 8)e5, hitting the knight with a tempo. After Black plays 8)...Nd5 moving the knight to safety, White can now play 9)Nb3 with a triple-attack on the d4 pawn. Black responds with 9)...Nb6 to attack the bishop on c4 and clear part of the d-file for the queen. White ignores the threat on the bishop and plays 10)Bg5, threatening the Black queen. It is best for Black to play 10)...Be7 to protect the queen (Diagram 9.6). After 11)Bxe7 Qxe7 12)Bb5, White will regain the pawn. A likely continuation is 12)...Bd7 13)Bxc6 Bxc6 14)Nfxd4 Bd5 and White may have a small advantage. The true battle begins with a complex fight likely to follow.

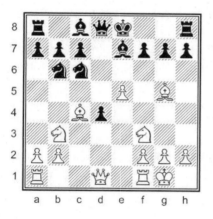

Diagram 9.6: Position after 10)...Be7.

No Thanks!

You may not believe this, but taking the pawn on c4 is not the most popular way to play. One way to refuse the pawn is to play 2)...e6, known as the Queen's Gambit Declined (Diagram 9.7). Black is satisfied with quick development and a comfortable position. 2)...e6 opens up the bishop on f8 but shuts most of the diagonal for the bishop on c8. If White plays 3)cxd5, Black will play 3)...exd5, and the diagonal will be reopened for the c8 bishop.

After Black plays 2)...e6, White's normal response is 3)Nc3. This helps pressure the center and has a possible idea of playing e4, increasing White's space. Black stabilizes the action in the middle with 3)...Nf6. It would be a worse idea to play 3)...dxc4 now because White will play 4)e4, controlling more of the center. Also, White will be able to win back the pawn on c4 with ease, leaving White with a desirable position.

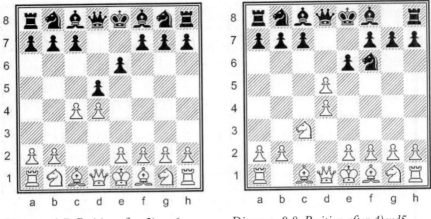

Diagram 9.7: Position after 2)...e6.   *Diagram 9.8: Position after 4)cxd5.*

After 3)...Nf6, White may have to think about doing something with the pawn on c4. If White plays the casual 4)Nf3, Black can follow up with 4)...dxc4. This position can become highly unclear, and it is not necessary for White to brawl in this style of game. White can try 4)e3 to protect the pawn on c4, but this may block the diagonal of the dark-squared bishop too soon. A solid and reputable line for White is 4)cxd5, known as the Exchange Variation (Diagram 9.8). Black's thematic move is the simple recapture 4)...exd5. {4)...Nxd5 5)e4 and White gains space.}

White would still like to play 5)e3 to help develop the kingside, so White brings out the bishop on c1 with 5)Bg5 first. In addition, White threatens to ruin Black's pawn structure with 6)Bxf6. If the Black queen recaptures on f6, White will play Nxd5. If Black plays gxf6, then the pawn structure is compromised. In response to White's 5)Bg5, Black plays 5)...c6 to keep an eye on the d5 pawn. Also, the Black queen is now free to capture on f6 if need be. Black would also like to develop the light-squared bishop to f5, helping control the e4 square in particular. How should White proceed?

Since Black would like to place the bishop on f5, White takes away that square with 6)Qc2. Black removes the pin on the knight on f6 and prepares to castle with 6)...Be7. Now White plays 7)e3 to help develop the bishop on f1. Black plays 7)...0-0 to protect the king and activate the rook. White plays 8)Bd3, forming a battery with the queen and creating a threat (Diagram 9.9). If Black does not react properly, White will play 9)Bxf6 and then 10)Bxh7+, netting a pawn. Black correctly responds with 8)...Nbd7. If White plays 9)Bxf6, Black will play 9)...Nxf6 while still protecting the pawn on h7.

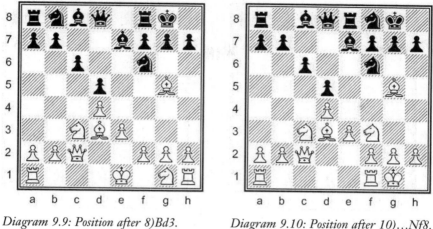

Diagram 9.9: Position after 8)Bd3.   *Diagram 9.10: Position after 10)...Nf8.*

When Black plays 8)...Nbd7, the most standard move is 9)Nf3. White has mobilized all of the minor pieces and is one move away from castling. All of Black's pieces are not in harmony, and the bishop on c8 needs air. Remember, the knight on d7 cannot move because White will capture the knight on f6 and then win the h7 pawn. Black tries a useful maneuver by playing 9)...Re8, and White plays the normal 10)0-0. Can you see Black's move? In Diagram 9.10, Black plays 10)...Nf8, providing a diagonal for the bishop on c8, and guards the h7 pawn from a new square.

Both sides have all of their minor pieces developed, and the fight for the kings ensues. They are relatively equal in regard to the elements, except White has more territory. This gives White a small edge, but Black still has a playable position.

The Slav

There is another way to decline the pawn after 1)d4 d5 2)c4. The move 2)...c6 is a weapon used by the cream of the crop, and it definitely stands by itself (Diagram 9.11). This is the starting position of the Slav—revolutionized by great Slavic players such as Alekhine and Alapin, influencing the name of the opening.

Black backs up the central pawn, remaining flexible to counter any of White's plans. White wages war in the center with 3)Nc3 (Diagram 9.12). This move is known to be the most accurate because it discourages Black from introducing the light-squared bishop into the game.

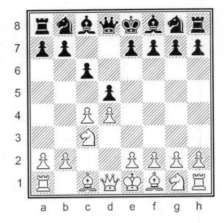

Diagram 9.11: Position after 2)...c6.

Diagram 9.12: Position after 3)Nc3.

The Others

In Diagram 9.12, Black has three alternatives to the main move 3)...
Nf6. Black can try 3)...Bf5, 3)...dxc4, and 3)...e6. Many times Black
has problems finding adequate squares for the bishop on c8, so why not
play 3)...Bf5 to activate it immediately? White can play 4)Qb3 when
Black has no sufficient way of defending the threats against the b7 and
d5 pawns. Black can try to diffuse the situation with 4)...dxc4, but
White will play 5)Qxb7, and Black will lose the c6 pawn after 5)...Nd7.
An improvement is 4)...Qb6, but White still holds the advantage with
5)cxd5.

If Black wanted to take the pawn on c4, shouldn't Black have captured
the pawn on move two? This may be true, but what about 3)...dxc4
now? This appears to be perfectly playable for Black, but Black typically
returns the pawn at some point. White almost always plays 4)e4, taking
over a significant portion of the center with the idea of capturing the
pawn back on c4. Black defends the pawn on c4 with 4)...b5, and White
plays 5)a4 to unhinge the defender. Black commonly responds with
5)...b4. When White moves 6)Na2, both of Black's pawns on c4 and b4
are hanging. Despite this, Black goes after one of White's pawns with
6)...Nf6. White plays 7)e5 to kick the knight, and Black responds with
7)...Nd5, helping out the pawn on b4. Then White takes the other
pawn by playing 8)Bxc4.

Typically Black proceeds with 8)...e6, opening up the lane for the other bishop while readying for castling. A continuation that has occurred is 9)Nf3 Be7 10)Bd2 a5 11)Nc1 Nd7 12)Nb3, and White has more wiggle room to operate.

Black can take another route on move three and erect a solid pawn triangle with 3)...e6. This also helps develop the bishop on f8. Although the diagonal for the other bishop is closed, that bishop usually has difficulties activating anyway. White has three mainly investigated moves. White can try 4)e4 (Marshall Gambit), diving head-first into the center, but this is risky and requires much analysis. If either side makes one wrong step, it could find itself in an inescapable trap. The evaluation seems to be highly unclear. The same can be said about 4)Nf3 because this allows 4)...dxc4 (Noteboom), and White gives Black an enormous amount of counter chances.

To avoid these cumbersome variations with multiple pitfalls, White can play the safe 4)e3 to protect the pawn on c4 to keep things simple. This closes the bishop on c1, but White must attend to the pawn on c4. Black mostly follows up with 4)...Nf6, and after 5)Nf3 the game has transposed into the Semi-Slav lines that are looked at next.

S.S. the Semi-Slav

In the position 1)d4 d5 2)c4 c6 3)Nc3, Black can play the reliable 3)...Nf6 (Diagram 9.13). This fits the elements fine because it develops a piece toward the center of the board while solidifying the d5 pawn. Should White just leave the pawn on c4 en prise? The highly regarded move is 4)Nf3 (Diagram 9.14). White plays a natural knight move that has influence on important central squares. Black can play 4)...dxc4, known as the Slav Accepted, which we dive into in the next section. For the moment we will take a look at 4)...e6, referred to as the Semi-Slav (Diagram 9.15). It bears this name because it consists of pawns on c6 and d5 as in the Slav, but it also shares the qualities of the Queen's Gambit declined, such as the pawn on e6. Therefore, it is only a Semi-Slav. This pawn move opens the bishop on f8 but partially locks in the other bishop. What's wrong with playing 4)...Bf5 first and then 5)...e6?

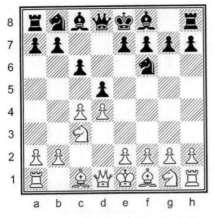

Diagram 9.13: Position after 3)...Nf6.

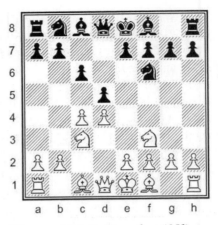

Diagram 9.14: Position after 4)Nf3.

Diagram 9.15: Position after 4)...e6.

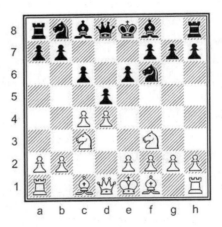

White can play 5)cxd5, and after 5)...cxd5 White will cause Black discomfort on the queenside with 6)Qb3. The pawn on b7 is put under pressure, so when Black defends with 6)...b6, White forces a concession in Black's position. Another move, 6)...Qb6, encounters 7)Nxd5!. If 7)...Qxb3, then 8)Nxf6+ exf6 9)axb3 with a favorable position for White due to the open a-file and extra pawn.

Let's look back at the position after 4)...e6 (Diagram 9.15). It would be ideal for White to activate both bishops, but whichever is developed first has its disadvantages. The highly theoretical and wild 5)Bg5 aims to energetically mobilize the pieces even at the cost of a pawn. Black can take the pawn and White can put Black under fire, but nothing is clear cut. Those who wish to voyage onto the endless sea, be prepared for your battleship to sink!

White could always play 5)cxd5, but after 5)...exd5 Black's pieces will be more liberated. Both sides will have a fine position, but White can keep Black guessing instead. White should throw the c4 pawn a life-saver with 5)e3. Although White closes the diagonal for the bishop on c1, material is saved. The goal is to develop and castle, then break the position open with a timely e4 simultaneously freeing the bishop on c1. It makes no sense for Black to play 5)...dxc4 because this helps White develop with 6)Bxc4. Black does better by waiting for White to move this bishop and then capturing the pawn on c4. Black can save time by playing 5)...Nbd7. White can play 6)Bd3 regardless, but this gives Black a chance to play the Meran Variation. As expected, Black plays 6)...dxc4 since the light-squared bishop has already moved. After 7)Bxc4 Black reacts with 7)...b5, expanding on the queenside. Black is able to gain a decent amount of space on this side of the board. How does White avoid the Meran?

There are lines just to avoid this, and they are dubbed the Anti-Meran. The most popular of these Anti variations is 6)Qc2. White plays a wait-ing game while keeping the flexible option of playing e4 in the future. Do you remember the nuance? If Black takes the pawn on c4, White can recapture with the bishop in one motion. Basically, it would be the same position as the Meran, but White has included the Qc2 move for free. Black does not have to take the pawn on c4. Black can follow the elements with 6)...Bd6 (Diagram 9.16). This develops a piece, helps Black to castle, and supports the e5 thrust, helping to earn territory.

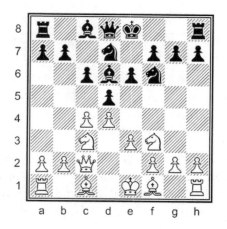

Diagram 9.16: Position after 6)...Bd6.

We are at a crossroads yet again. White could play the fun line 7)g4 (this is not a typo!), but it can only promise difficult positions to understand. I have played this variation with mixed results, but you don't have to bother with this stuff. Not all players who play from Black's perspective like to face this aggressive move, as it requires nerves of steel to play against. If you like to play these positions as Black, you must be prepared for 7)g4.

The practical 7)Bd3 follows the elements. It is unfortunate, but White slightly gives in to Black's wishes. Black continues with 7)...dxc4 now that White has committed the bishop. However, White was able to include Qc2 earlier, which aids in playing e4, and will x-ray Black's pawn on c6 when b5 is played. A logical sequence is 8)Bxc4 b5 9)Be2 0-0 10)0-0 Bb7 11)e4 e5 12)Rd1 Qc7 13)g3 Rfe8 14)a3 a6 15)Bg5. Both sides have all their minor pieces activated, and the rooks are connected. It's anybody's game from here.

The Slav Accepts

After the sequence 1)d4 d5 2)c4 c6 3)Nc3 Nf6 4)Nf3, Black does not have to close the blinds on the bishop on c8. The fashionable move among Grandmasters is 4)...dxc4 (Diagram 9.17). Black takes the pawn, and if White is not careful, Black will play b5, creating an overwhelming pawn mass on the queenside. Sure, White has the option of playing 5)e4, taking over the center, but this allows Black to hold on to an extra pawn with 5)...b5. How can White keep this pawn move in check?

Diagram 9.17: Position after 4)...dxc4.

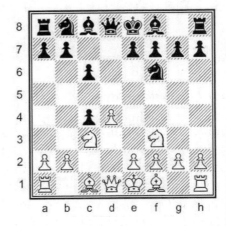

What about 5)a4? Black has to think twice before putting a pawn on
b5. White usually takes preventative measures against Black expanding
on the queenside first. Then White will try to exterminate the pawn
on c4. Black responds with 5)...Bf5, activating the bishop to its most
natural and effective square. White plays 6)e3 in an attempt to regain
the pawn while developing a piece. The bishop on c1 is blocked in the
process, but e4 cannot be played because the knight on f6 and bishop
on f5 work in tandem to deny access to this square.

Since Black has developed the light-squared bishop, it is logical to continue with 6)...e6 so that the dark-squared bishop does not feel left out.
White carries forward with 7)Bxc4 (Diagram 9.18), and Black plays 7)...
Bb4. Each side is ready to castle now. White plays the expected 8)0-0,
and Black brings another piece into the game with 8)...Nbd7. The next
task for White is to find the bishop on c1 a good home. It could go to
d2, but this is a passive square. To open the passage, White must play
e4, but White will lose a pawn. That means White needs to help this
thrust with 9)Qe2.

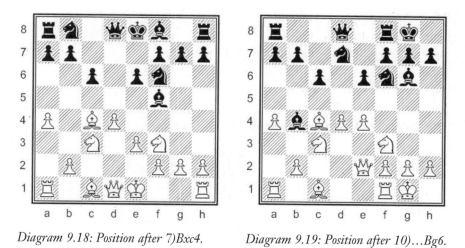

Diagram 9.18: Position after 7)Bxc4.   *Diagram 9.19: Position after 10)...Bg6.*

When Black plays 9)...0-0, White can continue with 10)e4, kicking
the bishop on f5 back. Most importantly, White seizes more space
in the middle of the board while liberating the dark-squared bishop.
Black retreats with 10)...Bg6 and threatens to win White's pawn on
e4 (Diagram 9.19). Black intends on Bxc3 followed by Bxe4. White
plays 11)Bd3 to defend the e4 pawn. Black responds with 11)...h6 to

take away the g5 square from White's bishop. White plays 12)Bf4 to complete the mobilization of the pieces and has a slight pull thanks to the space advantage. Black's position remains solid in preparation for a clash in the middlegame.

The Least You Need to Know

◆ Don't expect to blow your opponent off the board with 1)d4.

◆ The Queen's Gambit is not a real gambit because the pawn is often won back by force.

◆ Black should be very careful about accepting the Queen's Gambit while trying to hold on to the pawn.

◆ Be prepared for a complex battle with White or Black in the Slav.

Chapter 10

1)d4 Nf6

In This Chapter

- ◆ Everything begins with 2)c4
- ◆ The Budapest Gambit
- ◆ Benko or Volga
- ◆ The Benoni

In chess, there is usually more than one good move in a position. Last chapter, we saw that Black could respond to 1)d4 with 1)... d5, but Black has another excellent choice. When White takes over the center with 1)d4, Black should feel entitled to also gain space in the middle with the flexible 1)...Nf6 (Diagram 10.1). This move is quite logical because it stops 2)e4 and also oversees the d5 square. Not to mention, Black is only three moves from castling. This is not possible with 1)...d5. After 1)d4 Nf6, we will only look at White's most common second move 2)c4 (Diagram 10.2). In response, you will learn about some interesting Indian defenses on Black's second turn, which you may encounter or like to play for yourself.

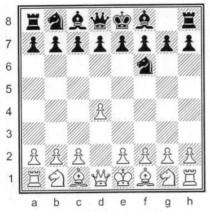

Diagram 10.1: Position after 1)d4 Nf6.

Diagram 10.2: Position after 2)c4.

Are You Hungary?

In Diagram 10.2, Black can play an interesting gambit, but if White applies the elements, White will gain an edge. The Budapest Gambit begins with 2)...e5, first introduced in a tournament held in Budapest, Hungary (Diagram 10.3). Black gambits a pawn, hoping that while White preoccupies him- or herself with defending the pawn, Black will develop pieces. White is hungry for material and plays 3)dxe5 to test Black's idea. In this scenario, Black has two knight moves, but the most direct, 3)...Ng4, helps attack the pawn that is now on e5.

Diagram 10.3: Position after 2)...e5.

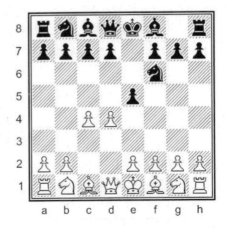

Watch Out!

In the position 1)d4 Nf6 2)c4 e5 3)dxe5, Black can try the tricky 3)...Ne4. It may be tempting for White to force back the knight with 4)f3, but this has devastating consequences. Black continues 4)...Qh4+, and White is forced to play 5)g3. Now Black can take the pawn with 5)...Nxg3. White is more or less obligated to play 6)hxg3, and Black responds by playing 6)...Qxh1, winning material. On the fourth move, White should not panic and calmly react with 4)Nf3.

After 3)...Ng4, White defends the pawn with 4)Bf4 while developing a piece. The game moves forward with 4)...Bb4+ 5)Nd2 Qe7 6)Ngf3 Nc6 7)a3. Black's bishop is under attack but plays 7)...Ngxe5, leaving the bishop en prise (Diagram 10.4). Can Black mock White like this?

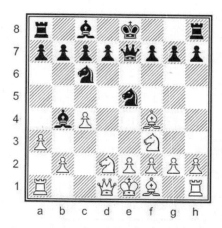

Diagram 10.4: Position after 7)...Ngxe5.

Diagram 10.5: Position after 10)Qd2.

White could take the knight on e5 first with 8)Nxe5 and then Black plays 8)...Nxe5. Then White could continue with 9)axb4, but Black will still checkmate White by playing 9)...Nd3#. The most accurate move for White is 9)e3, and Black no longer threatens to checkmate. Usually, Black plays 9)...Bxd2+

Watch Out!

In Diagram 10.9, after 7)...Ngxe5, White must not take the bishop on b4! If 8)axb4, Black can flatline White with 8)...Nd3 checkmate. Material is meaningless when checkmated!

and White recaptures with 10)Qxd2 (Diagram 10.5). All elements are relatively equal, except White has the bishop pair and a small edge as a result. Black still has a solid position, but White's long-term prospects are favorable.

Benko Gambit

Let's begin our opening journey from 1)d4 Nf6 2)c4. Black would like to distract White from his quest to take over territory in the center with 2)...c5. It seems as if Black is surrendering a pawn for no good reason, but there is merit behind the move. White could take the pawn on c5, but this does not help White develop. On top of that, White will be up a pawn but have doubled pawns. Those seeking accuracy choose 3)d5 almost exclusively. White gains ground deeper into the opponent's camp and prevents Black's knight from activating to the efficient c6 square. At this moment, Black wants to open up more space to freely coordinate pieces. One method is to play 3)...b5, known as the Benko or Volga Gambit (Diagram 10.6).

Initially, this gambit was called the Volga because of an article written on this opening in Samara, located next to the Volga River. However, the opening is more often referred to as the Benko because Pal Benko helped to popularize this opening by injecting new ideas into these positions. It has been argued that those in English-speaking countries prefer the usage Benko Gambit, while those whose native tongue is different use Volga.

Diagram 10.6: Position after 3)...b5.

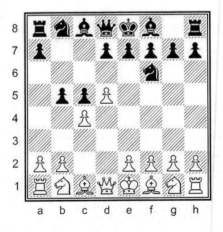

Incredibly, this gambit is still considered relatively sound, and it offers Black enough mobility to balance out the one-pawn deficit. At a glance, it frees up squares for the light-squared bishop, and as each side plays more moves, the advantages of the gambit will become clearer. There are various ways of refusing to take the pawn, but let's look at the positions accepting the gambit beginning with 4)cxb5.

Black continues with the standard 4)...a6. If White just sits there, Black will regain the pawn and have an open file for the rook to boot. White can give the pawn by playing 5)b6 and keep this rook contained, but we will stick to taking the pawn with 5)bxa6. There are three possible moves to retake the pawn on a6, but 5)...Bxa6 allows Black to earn the most space (Diagram 10.7). White plays 6)Nc3, helping out a potential e4 thrust. Black prepares to develop the bishop and castle with 6)...g6. White decides it's time to play 7)e4. Since the light-squared bishops clash on the same diagonal, Black reacts with 7)...Bxf1. The first point is that White can no longer castle after the only move 8)Kxf1 (Diagram 10.8). Also, the file for the Black rook is mostly clear, and the knight could possibly use the a6 square.

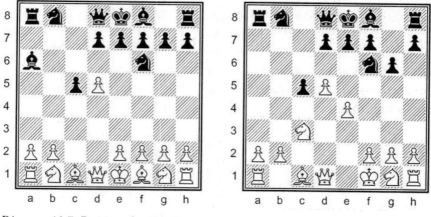

Diagram 10.7: Position after 5)...Bxa6. Diagram 10.8: Position after 8)Kxf1.

After 8)Kxf1, Black responds with 8)...d6 to garner control over e5. What does White do with the king? Not only can the king end up in danger, but the rook on h1 can become useless. White has unconventional means to keep the king safe while opening up squares for the rook on h1. White plays 9)g3, *castling by hand*. The game continues 9)...Bg7 10)Kg2 0-0 11)Nge2 Nbd7. White has created a safe home for the king and has netted a pawn. As compensation, Black has

Chess Language

If you cannot castle normally, you can sometimes re-create a similar idea. **Castling by hand** means the king takes a few more moves to position itself to a safe square, simultaneously giving the rook meaning. You may not reach a position identical to a normal castle, but it serves the same purpose.

control of more squares on the queenside, and this pressure will increase with the support of a rook or queen on b8. Also, the White pawns on a2 and b2 can become targets for Black later on. If anything, White has managed to retain a slightly more positive outlook, but by no means is White winning. I believe each side has reached a position that still offers practical chances to win for both sides.

Benoni

The Benoni, which rhymes with "baloney," is an interesting defense requiring an energetic set of moves to enliven Black's position. This position was first seen in a manuscript titled "Benoni," and that name has stuck ever since.

As in the Benko, the moves leading up to the Benoni begin with 1)d4 Nf6 2)c4 c5 3)d5. In Diagram 10.9, Black takes a different road with 3)...e6 (Benoni). The idea of this move is to weaken White's grip on the center. Black would like to take the pawn on d5, and when White captures back with the c-pawn, Black can stake out territory on the queenside with b5. The key response for White is 4)Nc3. The b5 and d5 squares are kept in check, and e4 is now playable.

Naturally, Black loosens White's center with 4)...exd5, and White accurately plays 5)cxd5 (Diagram 10.10). The other move, 5)Nxd5, would allow 5)...Nxd5 6)cxd5, and White exerts less pressure on Black's queenside. In Diagram 10.10, it may seem reasonable for Black to develop the bishop on f8 to e7 or d6, but both have their flaws. For example, 5)...Be7 is a huge error and a loss of time after White continues 6)d6, pushing the bishop back to the starting line. The other move, 5)...Bd6, interferes with the d-pawn going to d6, which will indirectly help activate the bishop on c8. Instead of these bishop moves, Black plays the solid 5)...d6, giving way to the bishop on c8. Obviously, White can't play d6 to hassle Black anymore.

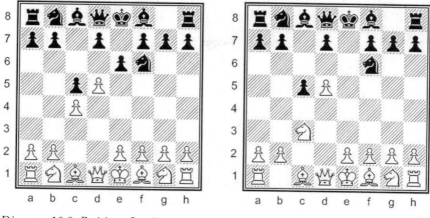

Diagram 10.9: Position after 3)...e6.   Diagram 10.10: Position after 5)cxd5.

The move that suggests itself is 6)e4. This is consistent with the elements because it helps White earn territory and opens a diagonal for the bishop on f1. However, this pawn can become a target down the line, and Black can sometimes expose this in combination with White's uncastled king. The game can continue quietly with 6)...g6 7)Nf3 Bg7 8)h3 0-0 9)Bd3 a6 10)a4 Nbd7 11)0-0 Re8. At this point, White's position can be preferred because White's bishop on c1 has more squares than Black's on c8. Overall, White has more space, and it is easier to move around.

Experienced players in this variation are not comfortable with little freedom for their pieces, so they try a more extreme approach. At the move nine mark, Black can play 9)...b5 to unshackle the restraints at the cost of a pawn. The move seems absurd because it gives away the pawn on b5, but Black can win White's central e4 pawn. Remember, I said that this pawn can become a focal point, especially with White's king still on e1. After 9)...b5, a common continuation is 10)Bxb5 Nxe4 11)Nxe4 Qa5+ 12)Nfd2 Qxb5 13)Nxd6 Qa6 14)N2c4. White has gained a pawn but has yet to castle. In the meantime, Black is already castled and is effectively up on time. White hopes to solidify the position and cash the extra pawn in the endgame. This can be difficult to convert, and I certainly do not recommend playing the White side of this position unless you are well informed and prepared. White can delay playing 6)e4 and avoid these long-winded variations.

The normal 6)Nf3 does the trick. White will develop minor pieces and castle, then play e4 at the most opportune time (Diagram 10.11). Black can't create any real counterplay by sacrificing a pawn by b5 because there is not a pawn on e4 yet. Both sides begin to unwind their pieces 6)...g6 7)g3 Bg7 8)Bg2 0-0 9)0-0 Re8 (Diagram 10.12). Now that White's pieces are mostly mobilized and the king is safe, it would be ideal for White to play e4 to take over more territory in the center.

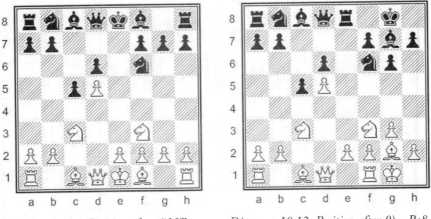

Diagram 10.11: Position after 6)Nf3.   Diagram 10.12: Position after 9)...Re8.

A strong knight move is 10)Nd2. White has three pieces that control e4 now, and the e4 pawn push cannot be stopped. Black must activate the queenside in the meantime. The usual move is 10)...a6. This pawn move will protect the b-pawn to reach b5 to have space on the queenside. White does not allow this expansion and responds with 11)a4. Black could move the light-squared bishop first, but it will end up being kicked back with a tempo. 11)...Bg4 will run into 12)h3, and 11)...Bf5 to 12)e4. Black could also try 11)...Bd7, but this takes away the d7 square from the knight on b8. Black develops another piece with 11)...Nbd7. A common continuation from here is 12)h3 Rb8 13)Nc4 Ne5 14)Na3. The battle for land begins.

The Least You Need to Know

- ◆ Black's 1)...Nf6 helps to develop and castle quicker while holding down the e4 square.

- ◆ There are many ways White can respond to 1)...Nf6, but 2)c4 is the main choice.

- ◆ White must be very sharp against the Budapest Gambit.

- ◆ Black must play for activity in the Benko and Benoni.

Chapter 11

The Nimzo, the Bogo, and the Queen's Indian

In This Chapter

- ◆ A champion's defense
- ◆ The once-popular Classical
- ◆ Not so bogus
- ◆ The Queen's Indian

There are many useful defensive setups to choose from against 1)d4, but what are the best? Well, the rock-solid Indian Defenses are confidently employed by many top Grandmasters. It seems that almost every Grandmaster includes at least one Indian Defense in their repertoire. If the best players in the world can't crack these defenses so easily, you should definitely feel more confident in these positions. Openings such as the Nimzo and Queen's Indian are constantly played in the biggest events, but no evident holes have been discovered. That might be for the simple reason that there are no real problems with these opening systems from Black's perspective.

Any Indian Defense begins with the moves 1)d4 Nf6, but don't get confused if the opening does not include the word "Indian" in its name. For example, although the Benoni is an Indian Defense, the name "Indian Defense" does not appear in the name of the opening.

Do you remember White's most common move after 1)d4 Nf6? By far, White's most common move is 2)c4, grabbing more territory. Now Black aims to activate the pieces on the kingside and bring the king to safety in a quick manner with 2)...e6. In this chapter, all positions will begin with 1)d4 Nf6 2)c4 e6 (Diagram 11.1). From here we will consider White's third moves 3)Nc3 or 3)Nf3, excluding the Benko and Benoni positions and transpositions.

Diagram 11.1: Position after 2)...e6.

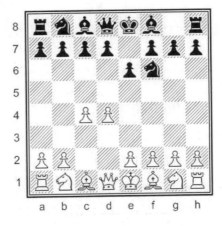

3)Nc3

In our starting Diagram 11.1, White pursues to strengthen the control over central squares with 3)Nc3 (Diagram 11.2). There are many paths Black can take here, but Black's next move is a matter of taste, so we will look at the ever-popular 3)...Bb4 (Diagram 11.3). Black battles back for control over the center and seeks to damage White's pawn structure with 4)...Bxc3+. In Diagram 11.4, White avoids any weaknesses with 4)Qc2, known as the Capablanca or Classical Variation. If Black takes the knight, White will play Qxc3, preserving the pawn structure. 4)Qc2 can also be a factor in controlling the e4 square. I do not want to seem dogmatic and tell you this is the only way to play this position as White. There are other good variations such as the Rubenstein {4)e3} or the Kasparov Variation {4)Nf3}, but they can lead to positions in which White may have to bear doubled c-pawns. Don't forget about pawn structure!

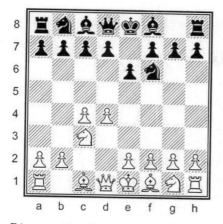

Diagram 11.2: Position after 3)Nc3.

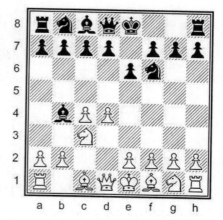

Diagram 11.3: Position after 3)...Bb4.

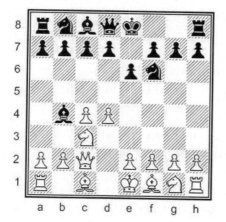

Diagram 11.4: Position after 4)Qc2.

The Main Line

We have looked at the position starting from 1)d4 Nf6 2)c4 e6 3)Nc3 Bb4 4)Qc2. Black has already brought two pieces out onto the battlefield, and it is a great time to castle without any more delays. The main move for Black is 4)...0-0 (Diagram 11.5). Black castles by the fourth move and does not disagree with any of the elements.

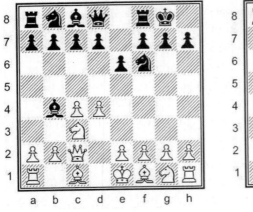

Diagram 11.5: Position after 4)...0-0.   *Diagram 11.6: Position after 6)Qxc3.*

The so-called "key" to the door is 5)a3, while it is debatable if 5)e4 is even a good move. Since Black's bishop is already on b4, it might as well capture the knight with 5)...Bxc3+. Black will have better control of e4 after White plays 6)Qxc3 to keep the pawn structure intact (Diagram 11.6). White is willing to play this position to gain the bishop pair. Black loses some control of the dark squares but has a plus in time.

At the moment, Black is not concerned about playing d5 because the knight restricts White from playing e4. Black prefers to play 6)...b6 to provide a few squares for the bishop on c8. White attempts to immobilize the knight on f6 with 7)Bg5, and Black follows the script with 7)...Bb7 (Diagram 11.7). The bishop on b7 is a laser that punctures through the center and eyes the g2 pawn.

Diagram 11.7: Position after 7)...Bb7.

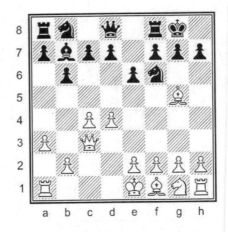

White plays 8)f3 to dull Black's light-squared bishop and to prepare to overpower the opponent in the center with 9)e4. Unfortunately, f3 is the most natural square for the knight on g1. You can't always have everything. Before Black plays d5, it is better to include 8)...h6. This dares White to take the knight on f6, but White would give away the dark-squared bishop. White keeps the pin on the knight on f6 with 9)Bh4. On the next move, White will play e4 without hesitation, so Black plays 9)...d5 to deny White from seizing territory in the center of the board.

It is wise for White to develop the pieces on the kingside before it is too late. 10)e3 is a good start. Another route is 10)cxd5 exd5 11)Bxf6. Black can take the bishop with the pawn, but the kingside pawn structure would be shattered. Black can boldly continue 11)...Qxf6, and when White takes a pawn with 12)Qxc7, Black just plays 12)...Ba6. In this case, White is up a pawn but is far behind in development. Black also threatens to win the pawn on d4, and White's position would crumble from there. This is a speculative line for White to play, and I do not advocate this materialistic mentality.

Let's begin from the solid 10)e3 again. Now Black completely mobilizes its forces with 10)...Nbd7. White tries to extract some advantage from the position with 11)cxd5 (Diagram 11.8), but after 11)...Nxd5 it is hard to do. The game unfolds 12)Bxd8 Nxc3 13)Bh4 Nd5 14)Bf2 (Diagram 11.9). If we evaluated this position with the elements, it would seem that Black has the upper hand. White is a bit underdeveloped, but White will play e4 and improve upon the space. If Black plays c5, White can also play Bb5 to activate a piece with a tempo. All in all, I would say that the position is approximately equal. May the best man or woman win! I almost forgot, or the best computer!

Diagram 11.8: Position after 11)cxd5.

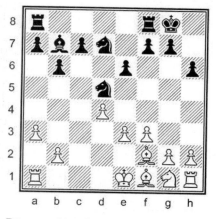

Diagram 11.9: Position after 14)Bf2.

You may have a few questions after these last moves. In Diagram 11.8, Black could also play 11)...exd5, but White will be able to mobilize more quickly. The next moves are 12)Bd3 Re8 13)Ne2, and Black cannot take the pawn on e3. If 13)...Rxe3, then 14)Bxf6 Nxf6 15)Bh7+ Kxh7 16)Qxe3 and White nets material. As long as Black does not fall into that trick, Black should be okay, but White has a small advantage. In the other line 11)...Nxd5 12)Bxd8 Nxc3, why doesn't White take the pawn with 13)Bxc7? Black will play 13)...Nd5, and after 14)Bd6 {an interesting sideline continues 14)Bf4 Rfd8 15)Bc4 Nxf4 16)exf4 Rac8 17)b3 Nb8 18)Ne2 Nc6 19)Rd1 Na5 20)Rc1 Bd5 21)Bxd5 Rxc1+ 22)Nxc1 Rxd5 23)b4 Nc6, and Black will regain the pawn with a slightly better endgame} Black is not afraid to play 14)...Nxe3. Then 15)Bxf8 Nc2+ 16)Kd1 Nxa1 17)Bb4 Nb3, and I would gravitate toward Black's position.

3)Nf3

Let's not forget, all the openings in this chapter begin with 1)d4 Nf6 2)c4 e6. We looked at White's 3)Nc3, but it is not always enjoyable for White to be pinned by 3)...Bb4. In Diagram 11.10, White plays 3)Nf3 to avoid dealing with the unwanted guest, the bishop in this case. No one said Black can't play 3)...Bb4+ here, and it is even thought of as a solid option for Black. We will look at this variation next. Before we do this, I would like to talk about a few possible deviations that can wind up crossing over to other openings. As in 3)Nc3, Black can transpose into the Queen's Gambit Declined with 3)...d5 or the Benoni with 3)...c5.

Diagram 11.10: Position after 3)Nf3.

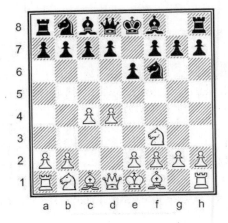

The Bogo Is Not Bogus

The Bogus Defense—oops, I mean the Bogo Defense—starts with the move 3)...Bb4+ (Diagram 11.11). I apologize to Grandmaster Efim Bogoljubov for making a joke about the opening named after him.

It is not at all a bad move, but it is just not the most popular third move. This brings a fighter to the battle and clears the remaining square for Black to castle. Overall, Black aims for fast and efficient development. White's obvious move is 4)Bd2 to block the check from Black. Black could play the simple-minded 4)...Bxd2, but White will develop while capturing this piece. Instead, Black plays the wily 4)... Qe7 and protects the bishop. This way, White may have to waste time to push back the bishop. If White takes the bishop with 5)Bxb4, Black will play 5)...Qxb4+ while attacking the b2 and c4 pawns. No matter how White reacts, he or she will have one less pawn than Black.

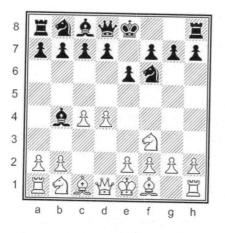

Diagram 11.11: Position after 3)...Bb4+.

The bishop on b4 can be a little annoying, but White should play 5)g3 and ignore the nuisance (Diagram 11.12). White plans to put the bishop on g2, where it will have a strong effect on the long diagonal (a8–h1). Black plays the normal 5)...Nc6 to fight in the center. This move supports the possibility of d6, then e5, to retake some of the center from White. The light-squared bishop is brought into the world with 6)Bg2. Black surprisingly plays 6)...Bxd2+, even though the bishop is not threatened (Diagram 11.13). The reason is to play d6 and not have to worry about the queen protecting the bishop on b4. If Black plays 6)...d6 instead, White will simply play 7)Bxb4, capturing the unprotected bishop. 6)...Bxd2 also sets up a positional trick. If White decides to take with 7)Qxd2, Black will play 7)...Ne4, and when White plays 8)Qc2, Black will continue with the intimidating 8)...Qb4+. Now White's pawn structure will be devalued after 9)Nc3 Nxc3 10)Qxc3 Qxc3 11)bxc3. Remember the elements! White does not want doubled c-pawns!

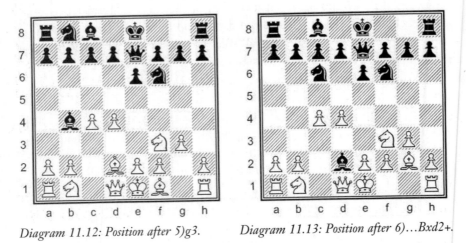

Diagram 11.12: Position after 5)g3.   *Diagram 11.13: Position after 6)...Bxd2+.*

In response to 6)...Bxd2+, White plays the smartest capture 7)Nbxd2. This knight aids the central e4 square and guards the pawn on c4. The move 7)...Qb4 is harmless because White can easily defend the pawn on b2 with the queen or rook. Black plays 7)...0-0, and White follows suit with 8)0-0. Black plays 8)...d6 to prepare the e5 pawn push, and White grabs more space in the center with 9)e4 (Diagram 11.14). It is logical for Black to continue with the planned move 9)...e5, but White can play 10)d5, and when Black moves the knight away, White can play 11)b4, gaining ground on the queenside. Black prepares for the future and stops White's intentions with 9)...a5.

White already has a space advantage but could try to grab more with 10)d5. Black can play the safe retreat 10)...Nb8, and the knight will soon come back into the action via a6 or d7 (Diagram 11.15). I think 10)...Nb4 may be a bit to promiscuous. After 11)a3 Nd3 {11)...Na6 is better} 12)Qc2 Nc5 and 13)b4, White takes over territory and pushes back Black's pieces. This can't be what Black had in mind. If we look at the position after 10)...Nb8, White has more space and a lead in time. However, Black will play e5 on the next move, locking up the center of the board. White still has a small edge, but each side should plan for the long haul.

Diagram 11.14: Position after 9)e4.

Diagram 11.15: Position after 10)...Nb8.

Queen's Indian

The Queen's Indian defense is a bit more subtle than the Bogo, but it is one of the most tested defenses played by almost all of the top 10 players in the world. In all openings starting with 1)d4, this is by far one of the most played. It is extremely solid and stays within the boundaries of the five elements. Black does not commit the bishop on f8 like the Bogo, but it plans to activate the other bishop with 3)...b6 (Diagram 11.16). The name "Queen's" is used to describe the move 3)...b6 (intending Bb7) for a queenside fianchetto.

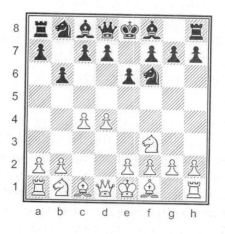

Diagram 11.16: Position after 3)...b6.

Now White wants to place the bishop on g2 to occupy the long diagonal to influence the center and x-ray the rook on a8. White scoots up the pawn with 4)g3 to accomplish this idea. Black plays 4)...Ba6 to throw off White's coordination. If White plays 5)e3 to defend the c4 pawn with the bishop on f1, it will defeat the purpose of g3. The bishop can't control those particular diagonals at the same time. White's most accurate move is considered 5)b3 to protect a pawn with a pawn (Diagram 11.17).

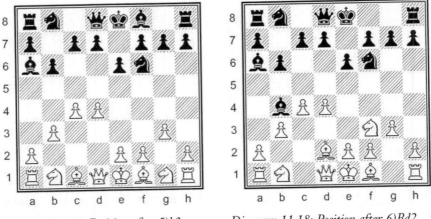

Diagram 11.17: Position after 5)b3.   *Diagram 11.18: Position after 6)Bd2.*

Black feels the timing is best for 5)...Bb4+. White should refrain from playing 6)Nbd2 because Black can force White into a corner with the moves 6)...Bc3 7)Rb1 Bb7 8)Bb2 Ne4 9)Rg1 Qf6. White can block the check correctly with 6)Bd2, but there is a certain vacancy on b2 (Diagram 11.18). White's bishop is ideally placed on the b2 square and the a1 to h8 diagonal. Essentially, this diagonal is somewhat vulnerable because there is no dark-squared bishop. Can you imagine what Black plays next?

Right now, White's bishop on d2 is poorly positioned. Black should not trade bishops because White will have an easier time mobilizing. Since White will usually spend extra time repositioning the bishop on d2, Black can afford to retreat with 6)...Be7. If Black trades bishops, this will only help White speed up his or her develop. Therefore, this move does not go against the elements. After this, White decides to develop the kingside with 7)Bg2 before moving the bishop on d2. This bishop x-rays the central squares and potentially targets the rook on a8. Black takes a precautionary step with 7)...c6, which also aids in playing d5 or even b5 (Diagram 11.19). These moves will ultimately help Black fight for more space.

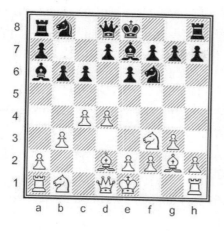

Diagram 11.19: Position after 7)...c6.

The normal moves 8)Nc3 or 8)0-0 are okay, but White would like to counter Black's d5 with Nbd2. How does White move the knight to this square?

White's bishop on d2 resides on the square that is useful for the knight, so White plays 8)Bc3 to give way to the knight (Diagram 11.20). It is beneficial for Black to continue with 8)...d5 to gain a fair share of the center while attacking the pawn on c4. Before White carries the knight on b1 to d2, White plays 9)Ne5. White pressures the pawn on c6 and lets the bishop on g2 see. Black should not play 9)...dxc4 because White will respond with 10)Nxc6, making use of the knight on e5 and the bishop on g2. Black is in a world of hurt, and it is impossible to avoid losing material. This is why White plays 9)Ne5 before 9)Nbd2.

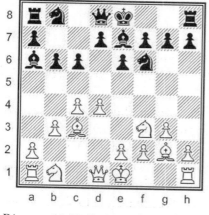

Diagram 11.20: Position after 8)Bc3.

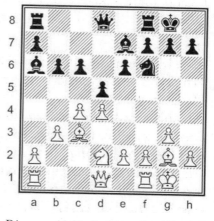

Diagram 11.21: Position after 12)...Nf6.

After 9)Ne5, it is wise for Black to dislodge the White knight with 9)...Nfd7. During this, Black must leave the knight on b8 to guard the pawn on c6. These knights are traded by the moves 10)Nxd7 Nxd7, and White plays 11)Nd2 to defend the pawn on c4. Then both sides continue 11)...0-0 12)0-0, and Black plays 12)...Nf6 (Diagram 11.21). Now White and Black are well mobilized and ready for middlegame. Are you?

The Least You Need to Know

◆ After the position 1)d4 Nf6 2)c4 e6, White's main moves are 3)Nc3 or 3)Nf3.

◆ The Nimzo and Queen's Indian Defense are some of the most solid openings in all of chess.

◆ If White can play e4 without making any concessions, this will usually lead to some positional advantage.

◆ You should look at famous games to understand more of these reputable variations.

Chapter 12

Hey Grunfeld, This KID Means Business!

In This Chapter

- ◆ The Grunfeld Defense
- ◆ The King's Indian Defense
- ◆ White's Fianchetto setup
- ◆ White grabs the center immediately

In the position 1)d4 Nf6 2)c4, Black can explore the hypermodern 2)…g6 (Diagram 12.1). The purpose is to move the bishop to g7 and castle in short order. Black's second move is driven by the principles, but can White try to exploit Black's sequence? White can play the very precise 3)Nc3 to tussle over the e4 and d5 squares (Diagram 12.2). Now Black has a major decision to make. Black can play the provocative 3)…d5 (Grunfeld Defense) or 3)…Bg7 (the King's Indian Defense).

Diagram 12.1: Position after 2)...g6.

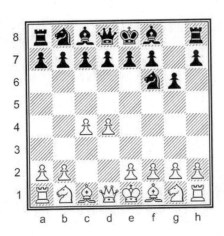

The Grunfeld

In Diagram 12.2, White strives to play e4 on the next move, but Black can delay this action with 3)...d5, as seen in Diagram 12.3 (the Grunfeld Defense, first played by Ernst Grunfeld). Black counters in the center and opens a diagonal for a bishop, but this move still has a price. White can cash in with 4)cxd5, and when Black plays 4)...Nxd5, White earns more territory with 5)e4 (Diagram 12.4). The pawns are a brute force in the center while the White bishops have full scope on the diagonals, even though they have not been developed. Let's not forget that Black's knight on d5 is in danger. The Black knight can fall back to various squares, but only time and space can be lost. Black should forego these retreats and trade with 5)...Nxc3. Then each side plays 6)bxc3 Bg7. White has a strong center but possesses an isolated a-pawn and backward c-pawn.

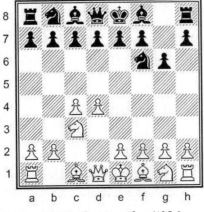

Diagram 12.2: Position after 3)Nc3.

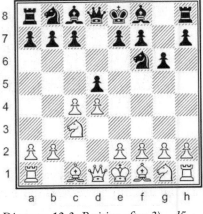

Diagram 12.3: Position after 3)...d5.

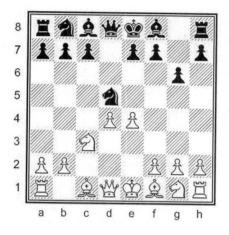

Diagram 12.4: Position after 5)e4.

White would like to activate the pieces on the kingside and finish castling, but in what order? The theoretical 7)Nf3 gives Black the option to play Bg4 and pin the knight on f3. The knight on f3 will have the critical role of protecting d4 down the road, but a bishop on g4 would neutralize its powers. White could play 7)Ne2 to meet Bg4 at any time with f3, but White will close the diagonal for the bishop on f1. This move lacks harmony and effectiveness. The fluid move is 7)Bc4 (Diagram 12.5). White develops a piece and makes Ne2 logical because it will not lock in the bishop.

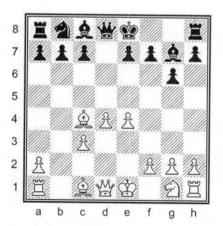

Diagram 12.5: Position after 7)Bc4.

7)...c5

In Diagram 12.5, Black could be content with castling but would like to lash out at White's center before it is fully supported. Black would also like to expose White's king, but that reminds one of the saying, "People who live in glass houses should not throw stones." Despite the fact that Black's king is still at home, Black plays 7)...c5 (Diagram 12.6). This threatens to win White's pawn on d4, but White reacts with 8)Ne2 to develop and defend. White should definitely not play 8)dxc5 or 8)d5 because Black will play 8)...Bxc3+ and take the rook on a1. This loses material!

Diagram 12.6: Position after 7)...c5.

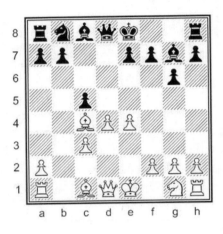

In response to 8)Ne2, Black develops with a tempo by playing 8)...Nc6. {8)...0-0 transposes into 7)...0-0, which is looked at in the very next section.} White's pawn on d4 is attacked more times than it is defended, so White plays 9)Be3 to add another guard. Black continues with 9)...cxd4, and White plays 10)cxd4 to keep the e- and d-pawns side by side (12.7). If White recaptures with the knight or the bishop, White will create an isolated c-pawn. However, in Diagram 12.7, White's king will be harassed on the a5 to e1 diagonal with 10)...Qa5+. White should not panic here. 11)Kf1 is a poor move because White will have a time-consuming task of activating the rook on h1. The simple move 11)Qd2 is okay, but after Black plays 11)...Qxd2, White must respond with 12)Kxd2 to avoid losing the pawn on d4. The queens are traded, so White's king on d2 is not unsafe, but it simplifies matters for Black.

Instead of 11)Kf1 or 11)Qd2, White can produce favorable complications with 11)Bd2 (Diagram 12.8). Black's queen is attacked and is brought back to home base with 11)...Qd8. Here is where the position becomes juicy. White's pawn on d4 is under fire from three of Black's pieces. If White plays 12)Be3, Black can play 12)...Qa5+, repeating the position. This means that if White plays 13)Bd2, he or she would have to be satisfied with a draw by three-fold repetition if the position is repeated once more. In the position after 11)...Qd8, White can play 12)d5. This move is baffling, but it is supported with concrete analysis. Didn't White just give up the rook on a1?

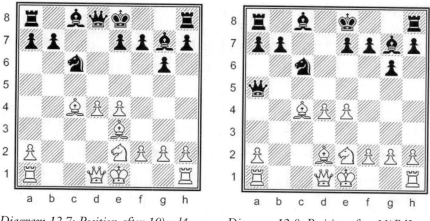

Diagram 12.7: Position after 10)cxd4.   Diagram 12.8: Position after 11)Bd2.

It is not advisable for Black to take the rook with 12)...Bxa1. White will take the bishop with 13)Qxa1, and notice that the Black knight on c6 and the rook on h8 are threatened. Black can try 13)...f6 to save the rook, and White will play 14)dxc6. After Black plays 14)...bxc6 the material is even, but White has a superior position. White's bishop on c4 prevents Black from castling, which also devalues the rook on h8. As a general rule, two minor pieces are better than a rook and pawn despite the fact that each group is worth six points.

As an improvement over 12)...Bxa1?, Black plays 12)...Ne5 to target White's bishop on c4. White should not play the careless 13)Bb3 because of 13)...Nd3+ and White will lose castling privileges. After 14)Kf1, Black could even gain material with 14)...Bxa1. Instead of 13)Bb3, White plays the resourceful 13)Bc3, pinning the knight on e5 to the bishop on g7. If Black were to play 13)...Nxc4, White would gain the upper hand with 14)Bxg7, dominating the dark squares. Black plays 13)...0-0 so that the king protects the bishop on g7. Now the Black knight threatens White's bishop on c4. White just plays 14)Bb3 and retains a slightly better position.

7)...0-0

Sometimes the simple path is the best path. If we refer to Diagram 12.5, after 7)Bc4, Black plays the effective 7)...0-0 (Diagram 12.9). Black castles before striking in the center, while White readies to castle with 8)Ne2. White does not put the knight on f3 because that will allow Black to play Bg4, pinning the knight. Of course, Bg4 fails to f3 with the knight on e2. Since Black is castled, it makes sense to play 8)...c5. White could snatch the pawn on c5 with 9)dxc5, but it just wastes time. Black can win the pawn back by force with 9)...Qa5+ or can ruin any chances of castling with 9)...Qxd1.

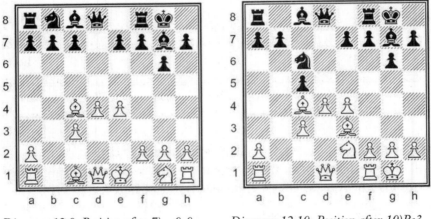

Diagram 12.9: Position after 7)...0-0.   Diagram 12.10: Position after 10)Be3.

8)...c5 does not threaten anything at the moment, so White plays 9)0-0. Black activates the knight with 9)...Nc6 and threatens to win the pawn on d4. Again, White can take the pawn on c5, but White creates doubled c-pawns, and Black can typically win the pawn back anyway. White is better off by playing 10)Be3 to defend the pawn on d4 and maintain the central tension (Diagram 12.10). A popular continuation is 10)...Bg4 11)f3 Na5 12)Bd3 cxd4 13)cxd4 Be6. Both sides are effectively mobilized, but White may have a more desirable position because of the better center. Nevertheless, current theory and analysis reveal that the only guarantee is a double-edged fight.

The KID

The King's Indian Defense (KID) is a great weapon at the hands of a creative player. Bobby Fischer and Garry Kasparov played the KID with great results. In recent times, Vladimir Kramnik dealt this line a crushing blow when he beat Garry's KID. Since then, it has fallen out of fashion amongst top Grandmaster play, but there have not been any proven reasons or refutations to the reputable KID. Only one player in the top 10 in the world shows faith in the KID, but he has excellent results against the top 10 with the system. His name is Teimour Radjabov, and he coincidentally hails from the same city as Garry Kasparov.

This defense has some initial similarities to the Grunfeld, but the KID usually leads to more closed positions and somewhat locked pawn structures. This also means long-term plans and maneuvers, which are not always so obvious. If you refer to Diagram 12.2, there is another choice for Black after 1)d4 Nf6 2)c4 g6 3)Nc3. The King's Indian Defense is launched with 3)…Bg7 (Diagram 12.11). There are multiple openings that include the name Indian, but this is specifically named the King's because of the moves g6 and Bg7 (Fianchetto). In the King's Indian Defense, Black has one immediate goal: quick development. White will typically grab the center with e4, but Black will be ahead in time.

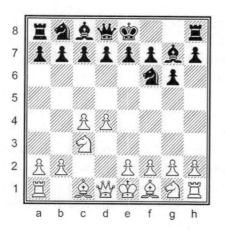

Diagram 12.11: Position after 3)…Bg7.

Fianchetto System

White's most principled move is 4)e4 right away, but can Black stop it if White delays this move? Not really. Before White plows through the center, why not develop the pieces and castle kingside first? This method has proven to be venomous if Black is not prepared. White can begin this Fianchetto Variation with 4)g3 in hopes of swift development while placing the bishop on a potent diagonal (Diagram 12.12). When White places a bishop on g2 against the King's Indian, it is typically called the Fianchetto Variation.

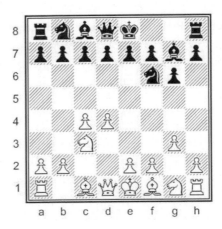

Diagram 12.12: Position after 4)g3.

The game very often continues 4)...0-0 5)Bg2 d6 6)Nf3. Now that Black's king is out of harm's way, a counter in the center makes sense. The main break for Black is e5, but it must be assisted by other pieces first. Black can either play 6)...Nc6 or 6)...Nbd7 to help progress in the center. I am not a fan of 6)...Nc6 because this knight can be kicked back with d5 later on. Also, Black can use the c6 square for a pawn where it will provide an eye on the d5 square. For these reasons, I give the nod to 6)...Nbd7 (Diagram 12.13).

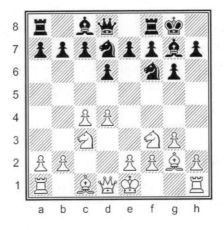

Diagram 12.13: Position after 6)...Nbd7.

You may wonder, doesn't the knight on d7 block in the bishop on c8? Well, the bishop cannot go to a favorable square anyway. If Black plays 6)...Bg4, White can either ignore it or play 7)h3. In these cases, if Black parts with the bishop, the light squares will become extremely weak, especially b7. Black could also try out 6)...Bf5, but White will play e4 once it is supported, pushing back the bishop with a tempo. At the moment, Black has no good uses for the bishop on c8, so it is okay to block it with 6)...Nbd7.

The common move here is 7)0-0. In this position, White and Black have followed the guidelines of the elements by mobilizing three minor pieces each and castling. I feel I need to mention that this position can arise from multiple move orders. This position can often result or transpose from the following moves: 1)d4 Nf6 2)c4 g6 3)Nf3 Bg7 4)g3 0-0 5)Bg2 d6 6)0-0 Nbd7 7)Nc3. This is just one possible arrangement, but don't form the habit of memorizing moves because you will get thrown off by different move orders. Learn the positions!

A response for Black that screams the elements is 7)...e5. Black utilizes the knight on d7 to play e5 and scrap for the center. White can vaporize the pawn with 8)dxe5, but Black will happily recapture with 8)...dxe5, and White has shed some space. White plays 8)e4 instead to have a larger presence in the center while taking away the e4 move from Black. It is vital for Black to play actively while White builds up the position. One plan for Black is to play 8)...c6 to help garner control over d5 and grant the queen a diagonal. The Black queen can go to b6, aiming at d4 or a5 with the possible idea of going to b4.

White's move of popularity is 9)h3 (Diagram 12.14). Any of Black's pieces that could potentially use the g4 square are taken away. Many times White will place a bishop on e3, and it does not want to be annoyed by a knight on g4. Also, after the knight on d7 moves, White would like to stop Black's bishop from going to g4 and pinning the knight on f3. 9)h3 follows the elements because it takes away useful space from the opponent. In response to 9)h3, Black can try to disrupt White on the queenside with 9)...Qa5.

Diagram 12.14: Position after 9)h3.

One key point is to place White under some discomfort if he or she develops the dark-squared bishop with a move like 10)Be3. Black will continue 10)...Nb6, hitting the pawn on c4. White cannot play 11)b3 because the knight on c3 will no longer be protected, so much better is 11)Qd3. Then 11)...exd4 12)Nxd4 Qa6 puts the c4 pawn under fire again. White can play 13)b3 to guard the pawn, but Black crashes in the center with 13)...d5!. Black is to be preferred here, as White cannot win the pawn on d5 because the c-pawn is pinned to the queen. If 14)exd5 cxd5 15)Nxd5?? Nbxd5 16)Bxd5 Nxd5, White loses a piece because 17)cxd5?? will drop the queen to 17)...Qxd3.

As you see, 10)Be3 is probably inaccurate because it can allow Black to free up its pieces. White should opt for the simple 10)Re1. The pawn on e4 is backed up, and the rook clears the f1 square for the bishop to help defend c4. Some games have continued 10)...exd4 11)Nxd4 Ne5 12)Bf1 Re8, and the game is dynamically balanced. It's anyone's game.

The Classic KID

On the fourth move, White can jump on the chance to take the classic center with 4)e4 (Diagram 12.15). White threatens 5)e5, forcing the knight to undevelop to g8. The Black knight can't go to h5 after this because it will be lassoed with g4. Good knight! Black's main move is 4)...d6 to hold back the e5 pawn push.

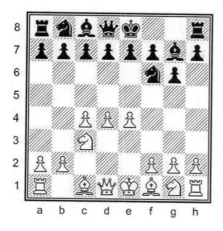

Diagram 12.15: Position after 4)e4.

When Black plays 4)...d6, the next moves are 5)Nf3 0-0 6)Be2 (Diagram 12.16). Black can respond with normal-looking moves such as 6)...Nc6 or 6)...Bg4, but why aren't these considered Black's best responses? I don't expect you to see Black's next move because it seems to blunder a pawn away. White is stacking up in the center, but Black needs to take a fair share. The epic move 6)...e5 is seen in Diagram 12.17. It's one of those moves where if it works, it's great! If it fails, the rest is obvious.

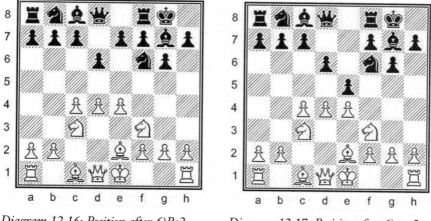

Diagram 12.16: Position after 6)Be2.   *Diagram 12.17: Position after 6)...e5.*

The move that is a fundamental test to the existence of 6)...e5 is 7)dxe5 (Diagram 12.18). It seems pretty clear that White wins the pawn on e5, but Black regains the pawn by pure force. The first step is 7)...dxe5. Then queens are traded with 8)Qxd8 Rxd8. Now White believes a pawn is won after 9)Nxe5, but Black has the resource 9)...Nxe4. White does not win a piece with 10)Nxe4 because Black plays 10)...Bxe5, and Black has come out fine in the opening. Since White will lose the knight on e5 anyway, why not play 10)Nxf7 instead of 10)Nxe4?

After 10)Nxf7, Black should not play the mechanical 10)...Kxf7. White will triumph with a net gain of a pawn after 11)Nxe4. When White plays 10)Nxf7, Black must find a way to evade capture from White's knight on c3 and then take the knight on f7. Black has 10)...Bxc3+ at his or her disposal. White plays 11)bxc3, after which Black responds with 11)...Kxf7. Black wins a minor piece for a mere pawn.

The Chess Sage

In Diagram 12.16, it is important for Black to find the right squares for his or her pieces. The natural moves don't quite satisfy all of the elements for some specific reasons. For example, 6)...Nc6 seems to be a helpful force, but it is easily sent back with 7)d5. Black should not play 7)...Na5 because it will be trapped after 8)b4. The position becomes a little interesting after 8)...Nxe4. The game moves on with 9)Nxe4 Bxa1 10)bxa5. The material is even, but the position is far from equal. White's minor pieces will overpower Black for territory and possibly decide the game before Black can make use of the rooks. After 7)d5, Black can try 7)...Ne5, but White will react with 8)Nxe5, creating doubled e-pawns when Black takes the knight. If 7)...Nb4, White pushes Black back with 8)a3. Of course, 7)...Nb8 is not what Black was aiming for in the opening.

Black could also activate the bishop on c8 with 6)...Bg4. The purpose of this move is to capture the knight on f3, which will help Black battle over the center. The reality is that Black will have significantly weaker control of the light squares.

As we've seen, 9)Nxe5 is optimistic but not so great if Black is versed with the tactics. A line that forces Black to be sharp is 9)Bg5. White pins Black's knight on f6 and threatens 10)Nd5 right away or 10)Bxf6 and then 11)Nd5. I remember the first time I encountered 9)Bg5. I thought I should just play 9)...h6 to force the bishop to retreat. I had a small oversight. White plays 10)Bxf6 and when 10)...Bxf6, White continues with 11)Nd5, attacking the bishop on f6 and the pawn on c7. There is no way for Black to avoid losing material, but Black should at least play 11)...Nd7 to protect the bishop on f6. That way, after 12)Nxc7, the Black rook has one safe square with 12)...Rb8.

Diagram 12.18: Position after 7)dxe5.

Let's return to White's move 9)Bg5. Black needs to demonstrate a defense against White's threat of Bxf6 and Nd5. The simplest defense is 9)...Re8. Black shifts the rook out of the pin, and if White tries 10)Bxf6 Bxf6 11)Nd5, Black has the cool-looking 11)...Bd8 to save the bishop and defend the pawn on c7. White's knight will eventually be kicked back with c6, and don't forget that Black possesses the bishop pair. The main continuation after 9)...Re8 is 10)Nd5 Nxd5 11)cxd5 c6 12)Bc4 cxd5 13)Bxd5 Nd7 14)Nd2 Nc5 with equal chances.

Refer back to Diagram 12.17. White's main move is the normal 7)0-0 (Diagram 12.19). This maintains the tension in the center and activates the rook on h1. 7)...exd4 only helps White centralize the knight with 8)Nxd4. If Black has the desire to kick the knight with 8)...c5?, White can play 9)Ndb5 and hunt Black's weak backward d6 pawn. This only damages Black's pawn structure.

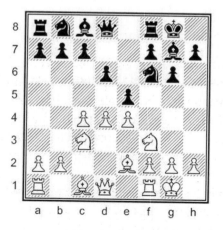

Diagram 12.19: Position after 7)0-0.

For years, Black's best has been considered 7)...Nc6. Black's goal is to trade the pawn and knight on d4 with White to decrease White's space advantage. Unfortunately, White plays 8)d5 to attack the knight and gain more space. Black retreats with the safe 8)...Ne7. At this point White controls more territory, but Black will soon counter with his or her own ideas. Since the position is closed, each side will use more time to mobilize their forces. For the time being, both sides have castled and have three minor pieces developed. The battle will begin soon.

The overall objectives for each side are to attack on one side of the board. Typically, White strives to gain more space on the queen-side, while Black will try and formulate an attack on White's king-side. White can grab space immediately on the queenside with 9)b4 (Bayonet) or venture into a popular line that runs 9)Ne1 Nd7 10)Be3 f5 11)f3 f4 12)Bf2 g5. Black expands on the kingside hoping for a crushing attack, but White will try and flank Black on the queenside. If White can force Black to defend, usually Black's forces will be overstretched and the attack fades. There are many world-class games played in this position, and I challenge you to look at these high-caliber games to get an idea of how the real war begins.

The Least You Need to Know

- ◆ As Black in the Grunfeld or KID, be prepared to give White a little more space in the center.

- ◆ The Grunfeld leads to more open games, while the KID ends up in more closed positions.

- ◆ You'd better know your stuff when playing the Grunfeld.

- ◆ In the KID, it is important to fight White's center with moves like e5.

- ◆ The King's Indian Defense can be one of the more difficult open-ings to understand. Choose wisely!

Part 4

Opening Choices

On the very first move of the game, there are 20 possible moves for each side and a total of 400 combinations of positions. This could make life much harder if you need to pick a direction.

In this part, you will learn how to choose openings that will suit you. There are many factors that go into this decision, but ultimately they should use the elements and have a good reputation. From here, you should test openings to see if they fit your style, and then learn games from the best players in these particular openings. Remember that the opening is just one stage of the game, so advance your knowledge in the others as well. Then you will truly be on your way to becoming a complete chess player.

Chapter 13

Building an Opening Repertoire

In This Chapter

- ◆ Deciding on the right opening
- ◆ Immediate victory
- ◆ Shock value
- ◆ The path to opening knowledge

In our journey of openings, many roads were taken, and all served as a learning process. Although some openings may be better than others, each has its own unique quality, which makes it one small piece of the whole game. This is all part of the history of chess. The greatest players of their time set the trends and led by example. From era to era, we build upon this knowledge that is portrayed by the best players of today. The overall point is that we should not try to re-create the game or construct entirely new openings from move one. We learn history for the same reason: to avoid repeating the same mistakes made by our ancestors.

We should follow in the footsteps of the best players in the world. I do not mean copy masters' games move for move, but use their ideas and concepts in conjunction with the elements. As openings and ideas change over time, only one thing remains: the elements. The elements will stand the test of time. Material, time, space, pawn structure, and king safety can be related to each and every move in some way. The only problem is deciding which openings to play. What is the best? What should be played? If I knew the exact answer, I could officially say that I have solved chess. Not even any of the World Champions can make this claim.

This means chess is still vast, and many ideas are still to be discovered. In the meantime, we have a solid foundation to work from (games of the World Champions) and elements to help guide us through the game. When choosing an opening, we would like to pick one that has a solid reputation and that sticks to the most principles. That way, we know that we can be more comfortable and confident with our choice of opening. In this chapter, we will discuss some of the better choices that you can use for your repertoire. Then you will be ready to battle in the openings!

Selecting Openings

Every person has his or her own tastes or styles. It is often said that the way we play chess is a reflection of ourselves. Well, for the most part this is true. People with shy demeanors often resort to simple and quiet openings to stay out of harm's way. Those who prefer balance opt for solid openings. Someone with an aggressive personality usually plays openings that offer the best chances to attack his or her opponent. Then there are players who are big risk takers, and they will play almost anything so that they can satisfy their thirst for a thrill. No matter where you fall in this spectrum of personalities, you should pick openings with a good reputation that you feel most comfortable playing.

Solid and Sound

There are so many openings to choose from, but it is wise to stick to the more reputable openings. If an opening isn't played much, it probably isn't that good. Although we only looked at 1)e4 and 1)d4 openings,

White can also satisfy the elements with the respected Reti, which starts with 1)Nf3. In the realm of 1)e4 and 1)d4 openings, either side of a Ruy Lopez (Diagram 13.1) or Nimzo-Indian (Diagram 13.2) is definitely a solid choice because there are no gaping holes. If the best players in the world can't crush these openings, it is not likely that your opponent will find a chink in the armor. Another reason is that there may not be any real flaws. These openings make use of the elements to the fullest and offer reasonable chances for either player.

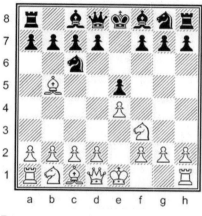

Diagram 13.1: The Ruy Lopez.

Diagram 13.2: The Nimzo-Indian defense.

The Ruy Lopez and Nimzo-Indian are not the only solid openings you could choose. Remember, your main objective is to reach a playable position where you have a fair chance to outplay your opponent. Some involve high risks, but you don't necessarily have to take these huge risks to reach a decent position. These types of positions don't necessarily cost you the game with one mistake.

Charge!

From the first move of the game, some have the intent of attacking as soon as possible. If you desire to go after your opponent's king, sharp openings are most likely the path for you. This means that both sides must play with more precision, and one mistake can sometimes be enough to lose the game. Basically, the more risk you are willing to take, the more you are rewarded.

Those who choose to go down this aggressive road should probably play 1)e4 as White. This tends to lead to more open games with a higher likelihood of an attack such as the game between Morphy and the Duke. What if you control the Black pieces? When facing 1)e4, the Sicilian or 1)...c5 can be a great choice (Diagram 13.3) This is a highly popular and excellent choice for those wishing to dive into early struggles or complexities. Instead of keeping the symmetry with 1)...e5, Black aims for an immediate imbalance. However, 1)e4 e5 positions can lead to some of the most complex variations in all of chess.

Diagram 13.3: Position after 1)...c5.

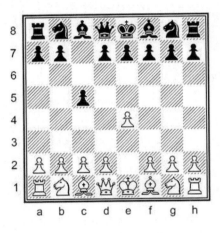

What if White tries to play into the closed positions of 1)d4? It is typically more difficult to open the position, but Black can still play moves to create confusion. The Slav (Diagram 13.4), Grunfeld (Diagram 13.5), and King's Indian (Diagram 13.6) are just some of the routes Black can take to reach double-edged positions.

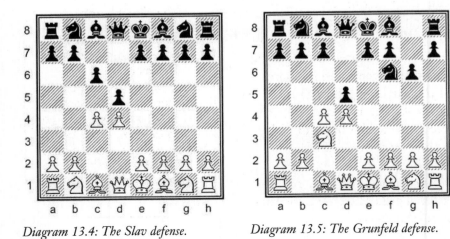

Diagram 13.4: The Slav defense.

Diagram 13.5: The Grunfeld defense.

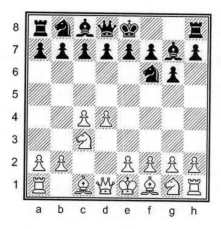

Diagram 13.6: The King's Indian defense.

Risky Gambits

The word "gambit" has a very similar sound to the word "gamble." When you play a gambit, you are rolling the dice, and sometimes the number you are hoping for doesn't come. In a sense, how the game turns out depends on how well versed your opponent is with the gambit. If you play a gambit, you are taking a significant risk. Nowadays, many of these gambits have been found to have some holes.

The reason I do not recommend playing gambits regularly is because you're playing hope chess. You are crossing your fingers that your opponent won't know the correct answer or even will fall into a trap. You may win some games, but in the long run, you will only hurt your development. What will you learn from winning the same way over and over?

What if you run into a gambit? The first thing to remember is don't go into panic mode. Of course, it is ideal to know some of the better responses to the gambit, but if you haven't seen it before, all you can do is follow the elements. A usual rule of thumb is to accept the gambit but avoid taking any extra material after that. If taking the gambit looks too dangerous, you can even give the material back to regain some time or development.

The Chess Sage

Don't play for tricks or traps! Play 64 squares! That means play the board objectively and don't play hoping your opponent will make a mistake. I am not saying all gambits are bad, but for the most part they are poor choices.

The Quick Win

It is every player's hope to destroy his or her opponent in the quickest fashion. Unfortunately, if your opponent is experienced, this probably will not be the case. As with gambits, going for the jugular with cheap tricks or traps is not a way to learn chess. For starters, you are just memorizing a sequence to win. Now, after a hundred times of winning in this manner, what have you learned? Well, my guess is that these opponents are beginners, and they really don't know any better. All you have learned to do is scout for weak players.

The most common way to win a game fast is the Scholar's Mate. Many kids are fascinated with this opening because it gives them a chance to win a game in four moves. If chess was this easy, it would not be as interesting and popular as it is now. So this "hope chess" variation begins with 1)e4 e5 2)Bc4 Nc6 (Diagram 13.7). Both sides have followed the elements, but now White tails off with 3)Qh5 (Diagram 13.8). Do you see the threat? Remember, every time your opponent makes a move, you have to ask yourself, "What is my opponent threatening?" White wants to play 4)Qxf7 checkmate on the very next move, so you should find a way to block the path of either the bishop or the queen.

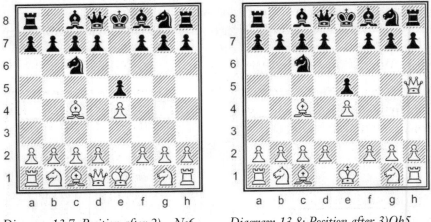

Diagram 13.7: Position after 2)...Nc6.   Diagram 13.8: Position after 3)Qh5.

Black could defend the f7 square with 3)...Qe7, but that suffocates the bishop on f8. Also, 3)...Nh6 defends checkmate, but the knight is poorly placed on the side of the board. Black's best is 3)...g6, kicking back the queen (Diagram 13.9). White responds with 4)Qf3, threatening checkmate on f7 again (Diagram 13.10). Black defends f7 with 4)...Nf6 (Diagram 13.11). A sample game continues 5)g4 Nd4 6)Qd1 d5 7)exd5 Bxg4 8)f3 (Diagram 13.12).

Watch Out!

Don't bring your queen out early unless you feel it is absolutely necessary! More often than not, the queen will end up being pushed back and sometimes trapped. Save the queen for the middlegame and endgame where the lady has more room to roam.

Diagram 13.9: Position after 3)...g6.

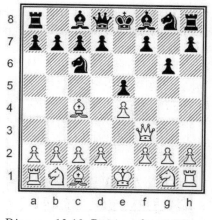

Diagram 13.10: Position after 4)Qf3.

Diagram 13.11: Position after 4)...Nf6.

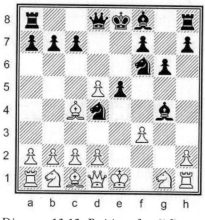

Diagram 13.12: Position after 8)f3.

How do we evaluate this position? The elements! Black has three minor pieces activated to White's one. White is up a pawn, which is doubled, and Black should be able to win back the pawn on d5. However, since White's king is so vulnerable, Black could care less about a measly pawn. Although Black's bishop on g4 is attacked, Black does not want to give White time to secure the king. The best passage to White's king is the e1 to h4 diagonal, but how does Black place a piece on this diagonal? Black plays 8)...Ne4! (Diagram 13.13).

Now Black's queen has access to h4 and the diagonal to the king. White should not capture the knight on e4 because Black will take the queen on d1. So White plays 9)fxg4??. White wins a piece, but there may be a little problem. Black plays 9)...Qh4+. White must respond with 10)Kf1, and Black finalizes the game with 10)...Qf2 checkmate (Diagram 13.14). White wanted to finish the game quickly, and this wish was granted.

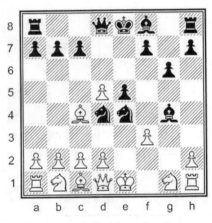

Diagram 13.13: Position after 8)... Ne4!.

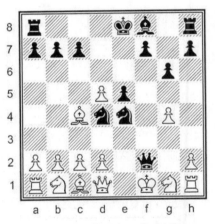

Diagram 13.14: Position after 10)... Qf2#.

The Effect of Surprise

All chess players use some sort of psychology in a game. We are all guilty of playing a move knowing that our opponent probably won't find the best move in reply. This goes against being objective, but there is a lot of logic behind this idea. If there is only a small chance our opponent will find the correct move or series of moves, then we are just playing the odds, right? This is debatable. On top of this, we can sometimes play odd-looking moves that will throw off our opponent.

Practicality

We already know that within the first 10 moves of the opening there are approximately 169 octillion possibilities. It is impractical and unrealistic to memorize these different combinations. That's why we apply elements to guide us through the openings. With these principles, we can come to a good solution.

On another note, sometimes you will purposely go into a position from which your opponent will have to play perfect moves to win the game, but if he or she slips once, that will be the end for him or her. It is hard to know where to draw the line. This is a choice only you can decide. I will say that it is often a poor decision to attack a piece hoping that your opponent will miss it. You can easily weaken your position, and because you are only looking one move ahead, you can overlook the big ideas in the positions.

The Long Shots

Once in a while when you play a game, your opponent will play something outrageous. It is not necessarily a gambit or sacrifice, just one of the moves that does not really listen to the elements so well. We have not looked at moves such as 1)b4 (Orangutan), seen in Diagram 13.15, or 1)g4 (Grob), seen in Diagram 13.16, because these pawn thrusts don't fight over the center. These moves are not *refuted*, but they allow Black to reach a playable game without too much effort. If Black plays accurately, White often finds him- or herself with a cramped position.

Who popularized these goofy openings? In 1924, Grandmaster Tartakower visited the New York Zoo with other chess players and asked an orangutan for the first move he should play in his match the next day. He played 1)b4 and the Orangutan was born! Its counterpart, the Grob, was conceived by International Master Henri Grob, who spent countless hours analyzing and playing the move in correspondence games. Do you really want to take advice from an orangutan or an opening similar to the one an orangutan suggested?

White will try these types of openings looking to surprise Black and travel into uncharted waters. Other than an initial surprise, these types of openings don't do much good in the end. Having success with such moves is a long shot!

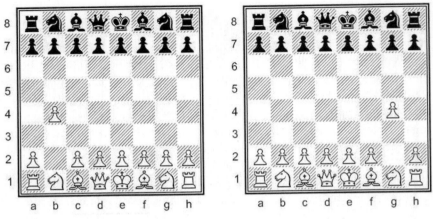

Diagram 13.15: The Orangutan.

Diagram 13.16: The Grob.

Chess Language

The word **refuted** means that a move or series of moves has proven to be wrong or just plain bad. In some cases, playing a refuted move will end in an immediate loss.

Inventions

Today, one can have access to databases filled with millions of chess games. Some have said that chess is dry, and there is not much more to explore because the game has been overplayed. Even though many ideas have been played, there is still room for creativity. Does it make sense to memorize the games of the best players? You could memorize some, but just copying them move for move can be dull. Also, no one said that your opponent will follow the same game. If you use your mind, you can possibly find a *novelty*, even in positions that have been played before.

Chess Language

Grandmasters are always searching for an undocumented move or **novelty**. Of course, there are so many positions that have yet to be played, but typically only new moves that have some merit are considered novelties.

Opening Improvement

I think it's safe to assume that the reason you decided to pick up this book was to help your opening play. More importantly, you must know the reasons why you play chess. Are you a casual player who plays for the pure enjoyment, or are you really serious but really lack in openings? Usually, the more serious a player, the more willing one is to study the game. Nevertheless, what you do with your time of study is the most important. Those who tell you that practice makes perfect are not necessarily correct. As Vince Lombardi once said, "Practice does not make perfect. Only perfect practice makes perfect."

Results Now!

I would be lying if I said I did not want to improve in the quickest manner. What if I improved quickly but hit a wall that I could not climb? Sometimes this goes back to the way you studied or practiced. You can study for quick results, but in the end, your development can become compromised. I have seen too many players who are worried about immediate results, especially through the use of openings. They spend countless hours searching for a way to gain a great opening position so that they can win on the spot or coast through the rest of the game. The ultimate problem is that no work is done to help develop the other areas of the game.

I could start a game where a beginner or novice begins with a great position against a Grandmaster. The Grandmaster will win almost 100 percent of the time, but why is this? The openings only mean so much if you are deficient in other areas of the game. Many can memorize, but not everyone is ready to understand. What you have to understand is there is no such thing as a quick fix; it is a learning process. If you learn the right way, you will find your chess experience much more satisfying and beneficial.

Learning the Right Way

The secret to learning chess is ... I will not make such a claim. There are many unique but effective training methods. However, nowhere will you find that learning openings is the only key to becoming a good chess player. Remember, you should learn the elements and other principles associated with them, but don't succumb to only copying openings move for move. In addition, you should study other aspects such as the middlegame, endgame, and tactics.

Your Choice

What are your intentions for playing chess? No matter what, I recommend trying out multiple openings to grasp the ideas of different positions. Of course, this is done by using the elements. This way, you will not be stuck with a particular system, and you will learn how to be flexible within the opening. I also want you to try out these variations before you look at famous games so that you can learn why your moves were or were not correct. Don't worry about losing a few games, because you will learn more in the long run. Feel free to experiment!

Once you have done this, you will become more acclimated and comfortable with particular lines. Then you can begin to look at famous games in the variation you would like to throw down. After this, you can begin to build your opening repertoire. Just remember, whatever openings you decide to play, use the elements and learn from the greats of the game.

Now you are ready to square away against your opponent!

The Least You Need to Know

- Stick to openings with a good reputation.
- Learn from the champions' games.
- Use the elements: material, time, space, pawn structure, and king safety.
- Don't get caught only studying openings.
- Expand your knowledge into the middlegame, endgame, and tactics.

Appendix A

Glossary

attack   The threat of gaining material or a checkmate.

backward pawn   A pawn that is least advanced within a group or island of pawns. This means that there are no pawns to protect it from behind.

battery   Two or more pieces aiding each along a file, rank, or diagonal.

bishop pair   When only one side has both of their bishops. The side with the bishops will typically have an advantage on the colored squares of the opponent's lacking bishop(s).

castling by hand   A king that has lost the right to castle but creates a similar idea of castling. White usually takes a few moves with the king until it is secure, simultaneously opening up the rook on that side of the board.

center   The four squares that lie in the middle of the board (d4, d5, e4, and e5).

classic center   When all four center squares are occupied and controlled by two pawns, for example e4 and d4.

combination   A series of forced moves, frequently involving a sacrifice, that leaves the opponent little room for error.

connected rooks   Two rooks of the same color working together on the same file or rank with no interference between them.

counterplay   A strategy used to combat a weakness or disadvantage in a position.

develop   A minor piece that moves from its original square.

diagonal   Squares of the same color running across a slanted line.

discovered attack   A moved piece revealing another piece's power that is aimed at the enemy.

double attack   An opponent's piece being attacked by one or more of its enemy pieces, such as a fork (usually done with a knight). Additionally, it can be where two pieces simultaneously attack two of the opponent's pieces, such as a discovered attack.

doubled pawns   Two pawns of the same color that are on the same file.

en passant   A French phrase meaning "in passing." A special maneuver made with the pawns when one side moves a pawn up two squares and the enemy pawn adjacent to it captures that pawn as if they were in a normal attacking formation. This is done on the fifth rank from one side's perspective. It must be done on the first available turn or wait until another en passant position has presented itself.

en prise   A piece that is left unprotected when attacked by the enemy.

endgame   Usually when the queens are off the board and all that's left are pawns, possibly rooks, and a few minor pieces.

exchange   When a rook is given up for a knight or bishop, the exchange is said to be lost.

file   A group of squares that lie on the same column starting with the same letter, such as the squares b1 through b8 (b-file).

gambit   Usually, a pawn given up in the opening for some type of initiative or positional advantage.

hypermodern   Strategy of chess that is in opposition to classical chess, which says that the center should be controlled by pawns. Hypermodern suggests that the center should be controlled by pieces from afar. Aron Nimzovich and Richard Reti were among the leaders of this theory.

initiative   One side having control of the way or the direction in which the game is going.

intermezzo   An in-between move.

interposing   A piece that blocks the connection or attack between two other pieces.

isolated pawn   A specific type of pawn island that has no pawn of the same color on the same or adjacent files.

king safety   One of the five elements that relates to how easily the king is attacked or protected.

kingside   All the squares on the e- through h-files.

line   *See* variation.

major piece   Rook or queen.

material   One of the five elements that basically refers to all of the pieces on the board. Each piece has a value, and if the total value of our pieces is more than our opponent's, this is usually an advantage.

middlegame   Usually, when both sides have developed all pieces from their original squares and are now jockeying for positional advantages.

minor piece   Knight or bishop.

novelty   A new move in a known position or opening stage.

opening   There are no defined boundaries of the opening, but it is considered to be approximately the first 10 moves where both sides mobilize their armies.

outpost   Where a piece such as a knight is having some influence in an area guarded by a pawn.

overextended   Pawns that have crossed into enemy land and are somewhat far from protection.

pawn chain   All of the same-colored pawns that touch each other on a diagonal.

pawn island   A single pawn or a group of pawns that has no pawns on either file beside them.

pawn structure   The way the pawns are arranged on the board. This is also one of the five elements.

piece This usually refers to everything on a chessboard except the pawn.

promote When a pawn reaches the other side of the board (the last rank), it may upgrade to a knight, bishop, rook, or even a queen. It is possible to have more than one promotion of the same piece (as many pawns as you promote).

prophylactic A move that defends or protects against an opponent's idea or plan.

queenside The other squares opposite of the kingside: a- through d-files.

rank Eight rows of squares going in a horizontal direction.

refuted A particular line or variation that is proven to be faulty or inadequate.

sacrifice When material is given up for some sort of compensation.

space One of the five elements that refers to how much territory or how many squares you control past your half of the board.

strategy A plan.

tabiya A position that is commonly reached through a particular opening. Once this position is reached, only then does the true game begin.

tactic To gain something tangible such as material or checkmate.

tempo A move that gains time.

threefold repetition When the exact same position arises three times in a game, no matter in what order or time this may happen. Then a draw can be claimed.

time One of the five elements, this also means to develop. The more pieces one side has developed, the more time it has.

variation A series of moves often referring to an opening.

x-ray A piece indirectly attacking a lesser piece through a more valuable one. The piece that attacks is located on the same file, rank, or diagonal as the lesser piece.

zwischenzug *See* intermezzo.

Appendix B

Advancing to the Next Level

Opening Books

The market seems to be flooded with specific opening books. You can find explanations of the moves or just a list of moves as in an *Opening Encyclopedia*. If you are looking to learn one opening, the work that seems to stand out is the *Starting Out* series. These books are written on the opening of choice, covering the key games and ideas. Even as chess moves are improved and theory evolves, the ideas remain. For example, *Starting Out the King's Indian* by Joe Gallagher is full of concepts that players up to master would find extremely useful.

Middlegame Books

There are many books written on the middlegame, but they do not necessarily tell you in the title on the cover. A couple books that do are *The Middlegame I* and *The Middlegame II* by the fifth World Champion Max Euwe. The first book discusses the long-term strategic aspects of a position, while the second reveals the more immediate gains of a position. Within each book, he breaks them down into specific categories of the middlegame, allowing the reader to organize the information easier within his or her thoughts.

I also recommend *Pawn Structure Chess* by Andrew Soltis and *Winning Pawn Structures* by Alexander Baburin. In these works, you will learn typical and somewhat systematic approaches in the middlegame when dealing with certain pawn structures. To be honest, these books are not really meant for beginners. I think they would be appropriate for tournament players with an approximate rating of around 1600 or higher. However, if you are not a tournament player or do not have any type of rating but you feel that you can grasp the information well, then try it out.

Endgame Books

The endgame is one of the most underrated and underappreciated aspects of a chess game. There is a myth that there is no need to study endgames if you can't play openings well or reach a reasonable middlegame. The reality is that studying endgames trains you in pure calculation and will help you see more moves in advance. Also, with knowledge of the endgame, you can aim for transitions of the middlegame to the endgame, which are technically winning positions. On top of this, if you play a great opening and middlegame to reach a winning endgame, it would be a shame if you could not finish the game and win. *Essential Chess Endings Move by Move* by Jeremy Silman does a great job with the basics of endgames that every chess player needs to know.

Tactics Books

Tactics, tactics, tactics! I cannot stress this area of chess enough. Players usually talk about how they need to work on the openings, but I hardly ever hear about tactics. Just like endgames, studying tactics can help increase your calculation skills. You will be able to envision the board and future moves much easier within a game. If you can plan out your attack one move deeper than your opponent, this can make the difference.

A tactic is a short series of moves that often results in the gain of material or even checkmate. In books, you will be presented with a diagram that will tell you what color it is to move and your objective. For example, a common format is "White to move and win." This would mean that it is up to White to find a way to gain material or checkmate the opponent.

There are many good tactics books out there, but I recommend *Chess Tactics* by Paul Littlewood and *1001 Chess Sacrifices and Combinations* by Fred Reinfeld. *Chess Tactics* separates the different types or themes of tactics with problems and explanations to compliment. *1001 Chess Sacrifices and Combinations* is divided by themes and is full of problems that can serve as daily exercises, which can help sharpen and improve your game. However, no explanations are provided.

Another piece of chess literature that I find useful for students and amateurs is *101 Tips to Improve Your Chess* by Tony Kosten. This book is very useful for hammering home the basics and is helpful in discarding bad habits that prevent a player from excelling in the game.

Chess Website: willthethrillaramil.com

For additional and supplemental material, you can visit my website: willthethrillaramil.com.

As you may have noticed, there are a few times in the book when I mention that you can visit this site for extra analysis on a position within the opening. I have found that some of this analysis may be too lengthy or beyond the scope of the book, but nevertheless, I have supplied these moves for your pleasure.

Also, at my site, you will find complete games using the openings discussed throughout this book. Additionally, I will provide any necessary updates and I will post chess problems for your enjoyment.

Index

T–U–V

W–X–Y–Z